RevisionGuide

KS3 Science

Collins · *do brilliantly !*

RevisionGuide

KS3 Science

■ **Ian Richardson**
Steven Goldsmith
Patricia Miller

■ **Series Editor: Jayne de Courcy**

William Collins' dream of knowledge for all began with the publication of his first book in 1819. A self-educated mill worker, he not only enriched millions of lives, but also founded a flourishing publishing house. Today, staying true to this spirit, Collins books are packed with inspiration, innovation and practical expertise. They place you at the centre of a world of possibility and give you exactly what you need to explore it.

Collins. Do more.

Published by Collins
An imprint of HarperCollins*Publishers*
77 – 85 Fulham Palace Road
Hammersmith
London W6 8JB

Browse the complete Collins catalogue at
www.collinseducation.com

©HarperCollins*Publishers* Limited 2006

First published 2001
This new edition published 2006

10 9 8 7 6 5 4 3 2 1

ISBN-13 978-0-00-721324-5
ISBN-10 0-00-721324-7

Ian Richardson, Steve Goldsmith and Patricia Miller assert the moral right to be identified as the authors of this work.

British Library Cataloguing in Publication Data
A catalogue record for this book is available from the British Library.

Acknowledgements
QCA (SCAA) for permission to reproduce past Test questions: pp. 42-49, 87-92, 130-137
'Coca-Cola ™', 'Coke' and the design of the contour bottle are registered trade marks of the Coca-Cola Company.

Photographs
Coca-Cola™ 23
Holt Studios 118
Mark Jordan 7, 23, 36, 78
Andrew Lambert 71, 72, 74, 75, 100, 104, 113, 116
Micropix Photo Library 60
Photos.com 10, 11, 12, 50, 72, 93, 123
Science Photo Library 7, 11, 14, 55, 63, 64, 84, 85
Paul Sterry 7, 9
Still Pictures/Mark Edwards 118
Tony Stone Images 31, 36, 52
Telegraph Colour Library 104

Illustrations
Sally Artz
Roger Bastow
Harvey Collins
Richard Deverell
Jerry Fowler
Gecko Limited
Sarah Jowsey
Ian Law
Mick Loates
Mike Parsons
Dave Poole
Sarah Wimperis

Every effort has been made to contact the holders of copyright material, but if any have been inadvertently overlooked, the Publishers will be pleased to make the necessary arrangements at the first opportunity.

Edited by Mark Jordan, Jean Rustean and Chris Davies
Production by Katie Butler
Series design by Sally Boothroyd
Book design by Sally Boothroyd, Wendi Watson and Jess Heath
Index compiled by Julie Rimington
Printed and bound by Printing Express, Hong Kong

You might also like to visit
www.harpercollins.co.uk
The book lover's website

CONTENTS AND REVISION PLANNER

CONTENTS AND REVISION PLANNER

Your Science National Test is about much more than just repeating memorised facts, so we have planned this book to make your revision as active and effective as possible.

How?

- by picking out the key topics by level (Units 1-3)
- by breaking down the content into manageable chunks (Revision Sessions)
- by testing your understanding every step of the way (Check Yourself Questions)
- by giving you invaluable practice at answering Test questions (Test questions)
- by making it easy for you to plan your revision effectively (Revision website)

Key topics by level

- This book is **organised by levels** so that you can revise the easier level 5 topics first and then move on through the level 6 and level 7 topics. This will provide a secure path through your revision.

REVISION SESSION | Revision Sessions

- Each topic is covered in one **short revision session**. You should be able to read through each of these in no more than 30 minutes. That is the maximum amount of time you should spend on revising without taking a short break.

CHECK YOURSELF QUESTIONS

- At the end of each revision session there are some **Check Yourself Questions**. By trying these questions, you will immediately find out whether you have understood and remembered what you have read in the revision session. **Answers** to these questions are at the back of the book, along with extra **comments and guidance**.

- If you manage to answer all the Check Yourself Questions for a session correctly, then you can confidently tick off this topic in the box provided in the Contents list at the front of this book. If not, you will need to tick the '**Revise again**' box to remind yourself to return to this topic later in your revision programme.

Test Questions

There are questions for you to try, linked to the topics that you have revised in each unit. You can try doing these once you have revised all the topics at each level. Or you can save them for last-minute practice just before your Test as a final check on your understanding.

Answers and guidance are given at the back of the book. As each question is linked to a topic in the book, if you fail to get the answer right, you can go back and read through the revision session again. You'll then be sure to answer similar questions correctly in your actual Test!

THREE FINAL TIPS

1 Work as consistently as you can during your KS3 Science course. If you don't understand something, ask your teacher straight away, or look it up in this book. You'll then find revision much easier.

2 Plan your revision carefully and focus on the areas you find difficult. The Check Yourself Questions in this book will help you to do this.

3 Try to do some Test questions as though you were in the actual exam. Don't cheat by looking at the answers until you've really tried to work them out for yourself.

ABOUT YOUR SCIENCE NATIONAL TEST

The Science National Curriculum explained

First, the technical information! The Science National Curriculum is divided into four Attainment Targets. These are called:

Sc1 Scientific enquiry
Sc2 Life processes and living things
Sc3 Materials and their properties
Sc4 Physical properties

Each Attainment Target is divided up into **level descriptions**, numbered from level 1 to level 8. (There is also a top level called Exceptional performance.) These describe what you should know and be able to do at each level.

By the end of Key Stage 3, the majority of students should be between levels 3 and 7. A typical Key Stage 3 student is expected to have attained level 5 or 6.

Exceptional performance	•	*Considerably better than the expected level.*
Level 8	•	
Level 7	•	*Better than the expected level.*
Level 6	•	*Expected level for 14 year-olds.*
Level 5	•	
Level 4	•	
Level 3	•	*Working towards the expected level.*
Level 2	•	
Level 1	•	
Age	**14 years**	

Typical 14 year-olds get a level 5 or 6 in the Science National Test.
This book will show you where you are and help you move up the levels.

What's in the Science National Test?

The National Test papers for Science that you will sit in May of Year 9 have questions that cover **all four Attainment Targets**.

The Test papers are available at two different tiers. The first tier covers National Curriculum **levels 3–6** and the second tier covers **levels 5–7**. Everybody has to take their tests in one of these tiers. Your teacher will decide which tier of papers is best for you to show what you know and understand about science.

The questions for levels 5 and 6 are the same in both tiers. You have to take **two Test papers**. Each Test paper includes questions in all four Attainment Targets and each Test lasts one hour. Both Tests start with the easier questions and get harder as you work through.

REVISION SESSION 1

Scientific Enquiry – All about Graphs

> **What you should already know**
>
> - The results of an experiment can be displayed in a lot of different ways.
> - Graphs and charts can be used to show trends and patterns in results.

QUICK CHECK!

Read and solve the clues below. Write your answers in the grid. You will then be able to read off, from top to bottom, another word to do with charts and graphs.

1. The quantities we change, observe and measure in an experiment are called ....
2. The variable that we observe or measure is called the .... variable
3. If we change more than one variable we do not have a ....test
4. The variables that are kept the same are called............variables
5. The line at the bottom of the graph is called the ....axis
6. A variable that can be measured to any number of decimal places is called ....
7. The numbers along the bottom and up the side of a graph are called the ....
8. When we plot a graph we join the points with a straight .... or a curve

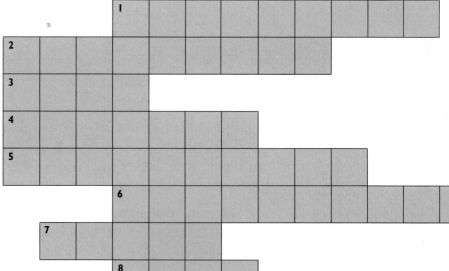

Answers:
1 VARIABLES
2 DEPENDENT
3 FAIR
4 CONTROL
5 HORIZONTAL
6 CONTINUOUS
7 SCALE
8 LINE

WHAT YOU NEED TO KNOW

CHOOSING SCALES AND AXES

- When you plot a graph of the results of an experiment, you must put the thing that you chose to change, the **independent variable**, along the bottom, on the horizontal or x-axis. The variable that you measure or observe, the **dependent variable**, goes up the side on the vertical or y-axis. Suppose you carried out an experiment to see how much force was needed to overcome friction and make a block of wood move. If you kept increasing the mass on top of the block, the results might look like this:

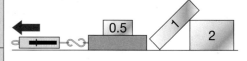

Mass on the block of wood (kg)	Force needed to overcome friction (newtons)
0.5	2.3
1.0	3.4
1.5	4.6
2.0	6.1
2.5	7.3

- The numbers or **scale** on an axis must always be chosen so that:
  - they go up in equal steps;
  - they enable all the results to fit on the graph;
  - the graph, when plotted, will fill as much of the paper as possible.

This would be correct:

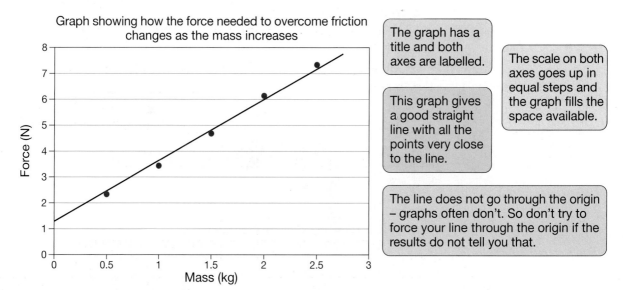

The graph has a title and both axes are labelled.

The scale on both axes goes up in equal steps and the graph fills the space available.

This graph gives a good straight line with all the points very close to the line.

The line does not go through the origin – graphs often don't. So don't try to force your line through the origin if the results do not tell you that.

PLOTTING LINE GRAPHS

- An experiment may have variables that can have any value within a range such as a measure of length or mass or time or temperature. These are called **continuous variables**, and should be plotted in a line graph.

When you have plotted your points then you should draw a straight line or a smooth curve joining most of the points, as in the graph on page 3. Don't join the points up like a dot-to-dot picture!

READING INFORMATION FROM LINE GRAPHS

- A graph lets us predict results other than the ones we actually measured. We can use the line to work out what the values would be between the ones we tested, and sometimes the results for larger or smaller values of the independent variable.

- The graph on page 3 could be used to predict what force would be needed to make the block, with an additional mass of 1.25 kg or 2.75 kg, begin to move.

WHEN TO USE A BAR CHART

- You should draw a bar chart when the independent variable is something like eye colour or type of plant which has definite values with no 'in-betweens' possible. These are called **discontinuous variables**.

- If, instead of changing the mass of the block, we had changed the surface across which we were dragging the block, then our **independent variable** would have been **discontinuous**. A bar chart would then be the correct way to display our results:

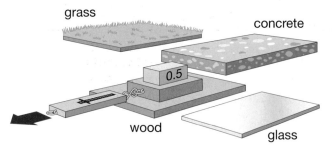

Surface	Force needed to overcome friction (N)
Wood	5
Grass	8
Glass	2
Concrete	10

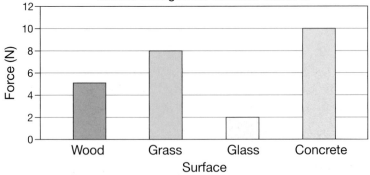

Chart showing how the force needed to overcome friction changes for different surfaces

- The bar chart needs a title and its axes must be clearly labelled. The scale on the y-axis must go up in equal steps and be chosen so that the chart fills the space available. However, you could not use this chart to predict values in between the values of the independent variable as there is not a sensible value in between glass and concrete, for example.

- A graph lets us see the relationship between the variables. If you are asked to describe what the graph shows, you must use the correct words.

- In the example from page 3, you could say that heavier blocks are harder to move – this would be a very simple explanation of what you saw and found out in your experiment. However, the correct explanation of the relationship would be to say that 'as the mass of the block increases, so the force needed to overcome friction increases'.

CHECK YOURSELF QUESTIONS

Q1 Complete this table to show the total stopping distance of a vehicle moving at speeds between 20 and 70 miles per hour.

Total stopping distance = thinking distance + braking distance

9 m thinking distance   14 m braking distance

30 MPH

Speed of car (miles per hour)	Driver's thinking distance (m)	Braking distance (m)	Total stopping distance (m)
20	6	6	
30	9	14	
40	12	24	
50	15	38	
60	18	55	
70	21	75	

Q2 Draw a graph on a separate sheet of paper to show how the speed of the car affects the total stopping distance. Then, from your graph find the total stopping distance at 45 mph .... and at 65 mph ....

Q3 Sort these variables into continuous and discontinuous.

Shoe size
Hand span
Length of little finger
Height
Eye colour
Gender
Hair colour

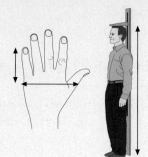

Classification

What you should already know

- Living things can be put into groups using keys based on observable features.

- There are many different types of living things.

QUICK CHECK!
Try this 'crosstick' puzzle. It contains the names of individual animals or groups of animals that have backbones.

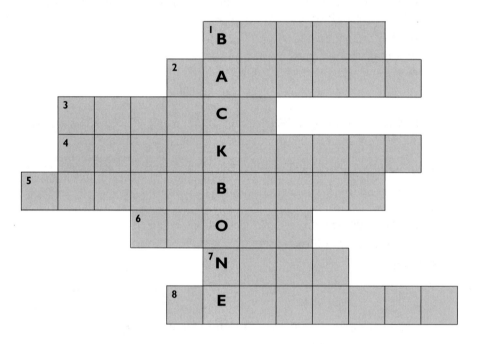

1 Animals that have feathers. Most of them can fly.
2 The group that includes humans, dogs and cats.
3 A flat fish that you can eat with chips.
4 Very dark coloured birds often seen in gardens.
5 The group of animals that live in both water and on land, and includes frogs and toads.
6 A freshwater fish that is caught by fly fishing and is often farmed for eating.
7 A British amphibian that has four legs and a tail (unlike frogs and toads).
8 Lizards, crocodiles and snakes belong to this group.

Answers:
1 BIRDS 2 MAMMALS
3 PLAICE 4 BLACKBIRDS
5 AMPHIBIANS 6 TROUT
7 NEWT 8 REPTILES

WHAT YOU NEED TO KNOW

- Scientists sort living things into **groups**. The members of each group have similar features. The process of sorting things into groups is called **classification**. Classification enables scientists to understand the relationships between living things.

- Although no two human beings are exactly the same, they all have many features in common. For example, the human body has two legs for walking on, two arms, a skeleton inside their body, and so on.

- A group of organisms that have many similar features and that can successfully interbreed is called a **species**. For example, cats are one species and dogs are another species.

- Different species that are quite similar to each other can be put into larger **groups**. For example, although tigers and rats are very different, both species have the following features in common:
  - hair on their skin;
  - the mothers feed their young with their own milk;
  - they have backbones;
  - they give birth to live babies;
  - they are warm blooded.

- Members of the group with these features are collected together and called **mammals**. Human beings are also mammals.

- We can divide up all the living things on Earth into five kingdoms:
  1 Animal kingdom
  2 Plant kingdom
  3 Prokaryotes (which include bacteria)
  4 Protoctista (single-celled organisms)
  5 Fungi

- The branching diagram below shows how the animal kingdom is divided up. The first big division within the animal kingdom is based on whether or not the animals have a backbone. Animals that have a backbone are called **vertebrates** and animals that do not have a backbone are called **invertebrates**.

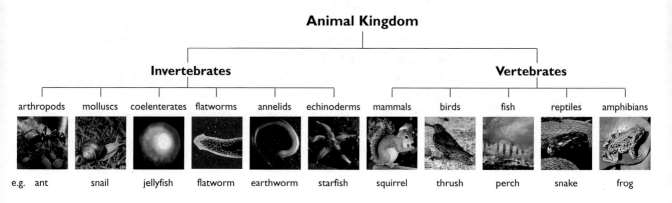

Animal Kingdom

Invertebrates

arthropods	molluscs	coelenterates	flatworms	annelids	echinoderms
e.g. ant	snail	jellyfish	flatworm	earthworm	starfish

Vertebrates

mammals	birds	fish	reptiles	amphibians
squirrel	thrush	perch	snake	frog

- Although vertebrates all have a backbone, each group within the vertebrates has special features in common that make it very different from the other groups. Look at the vertebrate fact file below to see why the different vertebrates are grouped in the way they are.

VERTEBRATES

Group	Features they have in common
Amphibians	smooth damp skin, live on land and in water, lay soft eggs in water
Birds	feathers, lay hard-shelled eggs on land
Fish	scales, fins and gills
Mammals	hair or fur, young feed on mother's milk
Reptiles	hard dry scales, lay soft-shelled eggs on land

- The fact file below shows the main groups of invertebrates and the important features that members of each group have in common.

INVERTEBRATES

Group	Features they have in common	Examples
Coelenterates	jelly-like, gut has only one opening, live in water, radially symmetrical	jelly fish
Echinoderms	hard outer skeleton often with spines, five sections to the body	starfish, sea urchin
Arthropods	jointed legs and an external skeleton	insects, crabs and spiders
Flatworms	flat bodied worms, many without sections, have a mouth but no anus	tapeworms
Annelids	worms with segmented bodies	earthworms
Molluscs	soft bodied, no segments, many have a hard shell	snails and slugs

- The plant kingdom is organised in a similar way. The first two large groups within the plant kingdom are plants that make seeds and plants that do not make seeds (seedless). The plants that have seeds belong to one of two groups – either flowering plants or conifers. The diagram below shows how the plant kingdom is divided up.

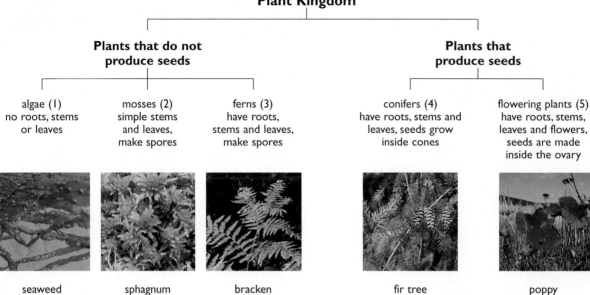

Plant Kingdom

Plants that do not produce seeds

- algae (1) no roots, stems or leaves
- mosses (2) simple stems and leaves, make spores
- ferns (3) have roots, stems and leaves, make spores

Plants that produce seeds

- conifers (4) have roots, stems and leaves, seeds grow inside cones
- flowering plants (5) have roots, stems, leaves and flowers, seeds are made inside the ovary

e.g.   seaweed   sphagnum   bracken   fir tree   poppy

Q1 Complete the table about invertebrates.

Name of invertebrate	Group it belongs to
Spider	arthropod
Slug	
Jelly fish	
Tapeworm	
Earthworm	

Q2 List the five groups of vertebrates and write a sentence or two about each group, describing what the members of that group have in common.

Q3 Copy and complete this table showing the features that different plant groups have in common.

Group	Things they have in common	Example
Algae	no roots, stems or leaves	seaweed
Mosses		
Ferns		
Conifers		
Flowering plants		

Habitat and Adaptation

What you should already know

- Where an animal lives is called its habitat.

- A habitat is made up of all the plants and other animals that live there and takes account of other environmental factors such as weather conditions and air pollution.

QUICK CHECK!

Find the names of 12 plants and animals in this word search and decide which would live in a woodland habitat and which in a pond habitat.

W	A	T	E	R	F	L	E	A	K	L	X
A	S	Q	U	I	R	R	E	L	F	B	E
F	W	V	G	T	I	B	B	A	R	F	N
A	P	L	A	N	K	T	O	N	P	T	G
X	C	A	T	E	R	P	I	L	L	A	R
L	A	F	M	V	J	W	T	B	N	D	A
E	R	R	O	A	K	T	R	E	E	P	S
E	P	B	U	V	T	U	I	O	L	O	S
C	G	T	S	E	Y	F	R	O	G	L	Z
H	R	W	E	R	G	J	K	S	A	E	X

WOODLAND	POND

WHAT YOU NEED TO KNOW

ADAPTATION

- Plants and animals can adapt to enable them to live in their habitat. This happens over many generations and takes a very long time. It happens because the organisms with characteristics suited to the habitat are the ones which survive best. When they breed, their characteristics are passed on so that their offspring will be adapted to their surroundings.

- These characteristics can be ones that enable them:
    - to avoid predators;
    - to survive extreme conditions of weather or light;
    - to find food more easily.

- Think of a polar bear.
    - White fur is good camouflage to enable the bears to avoid predators.
    - Thick fur helps retain body heat in cold conditions.
    - Sharp claws grip icy surfaces well.
    - Long strong legs mean that long distances can be covered and at high speed.
    - Strong teeth are good for catching and killing prey.

DAILY AND SEASONAL ADAPTATIONS

- Some adaptations can enable animals and plants to cope with changes in their habitat through the day or the year.

- Some animals sleep in the day and hunt for their food at night. Some flowers close up at night when there is no light and it is colder than in the day.

- Animals who **hibernate** sleep all through the winter, when food is in short supply, and wake up for the summer.

- Deciduous trees lose their leaves in winter. In winter there is little sunlight for photosynthesis so it is not possible to make much food. The plant therefore stops growing and producing flowers and fruit.

? CHECK YOURSELF QUESTIONS

Q1 Give three ways in which cactus plants are adapted to their habitat.

a ....

b ....

c ....

Q2 Imagine you could set out to design a mammal from scratch! This mammal has to be able to live in a habitat where in the summer it is very hot and dry and in the winter it becomes cold and wet. You must decide whether your mammal should be a herbivore or a carnivore. Give five characteristics that your mammal would have and a reason for each.

Characteristic	Reason

What you should already know

- The scientific names of some major organs in the human body.

- The position of these organs in the human body.

- Body systems are made up of several organs.

QUICK CHECK!

Some of the organs in the human body work together and are part of an organ system, for example, the digestive system.
Solve the clues below to give the names of organs, parts or functions (jobs) of the digestive system.

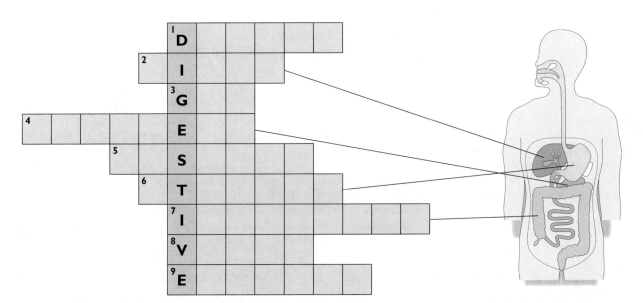

1   To break down food.
2   The largest internal organ in the body, it is red/brown.
3   The tube which forms the digestive system.
4   Gland that releases digestive juices into the small intestine.
5   The small intestine does this to digested food.
6   Food is stored here and mixed with digestive juices before moving into the intestine.
7   There is a small one and a large one.
8   Tiny finger-like things that help the small intestine absorb food.
9   Important chemicals that help to break down large food molecules.

Answers:
1 DIGEST 2 LIVER
3 GUT 4 PANCREAS
5 ABSORBS 6 STOMACH
7 INTESTINE 8 VILLI
9 ENZYMES

WHAT YOU NEED TO KNOW

- Four of the organ systems in the body are: the circulatory system, the reproductive system, the digestive system and the respiratory system.

- The main organs of the respiratory system are the lungs; these are the organs that allow oxygen to be absorbed into the blood. We will deal with respiration in greater detail in the *Respiration Revision Session* on pages 103–105.

- This chapter looks at the function (job) of organs in the three other systems.

THE DIGESTIVE SYSTEM

- The function of the digestive system is to break down insoluble food into small particles of food that can dissolve. Only after they are broken down can the dissolved food be absorbed through the intestine wall into the bloodstream. The breakdown of food in this way is called digestion.

- The organs of the digestive system have different jobs. They may help in:
  - breaking down the food;
  - carrying food from one place to another;
  - absorbing the food.

- Each organ in the digestive system (and other systems) is well suited to doing its job. We say that the organs are well **adapted**. The table below lists some organs that are part of the digestive system and their functions.

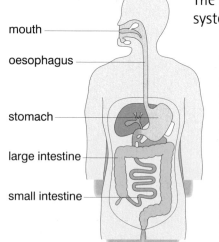

mouth
oesophagus
stomach
large intestine
small intestine

Organ	Main functions in digestion
mouth	teeth break down food into smaller pieces; saliva starts breakdown of starch
oesophagus (food tube/gullet)	carries food from the mouth to the stomach
stomach	starts breakdown of protein
small intestine	digests fat; completes digestion of protein and starch; absorbs digested food into bloodstream
large intestine	absorbs water into bloodstream from the indigestible food that is left

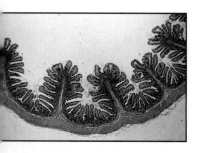

- The photograph on the left shows the lining of the small intestine. It is covered with tiny finger-like projections called **villi**. These make the surface area of the small intestine wall much larger and make it better at absorbing the digested food.

THE CIRCULATORY SYSTEM

- The circulatory system is made up of a set of organs whose main function is to ensure the circulation of the blood around the body. Just like the digestive system, it is made up of organs that each have a particular function.

- The organs of the circulatory system help to:
  - defend the body against disease;
  - carry oxygen, carbon dioxide, digested food and waste products around the body.

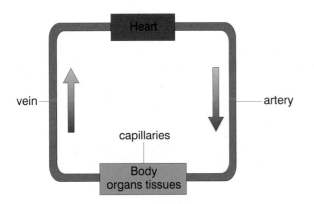

Organ	Main function in circulation
heart	pumps blood around body
capillary	releases useful substances to tissues and absorbs waste materials
artery	carries blood at high pressure away from the heart
vein	carries blood at low pressure back to the heart

- The blood is made up of different parts to carry out its functions:

Blood part	Function
red cells	carry oxygen
white cells	kill bacteria and viruses, defend body against disease
plasma	carries carbon dioxide, digested food and many other dissolved substances

THE REPRODUCTIVE SYSTEM

- The organs of the reproductive system are shown in the table below. The organs are listed with their main functions.

Organ	Main function in reproduction
uterus	this is where the baby develops
penis	it becomes erect to be pushed into the vagina and deposit sperm inside the female's body
ovaries	these two organs in the female body release an ovum (egg) each month
placenta	the organ which allows food and oxygen to pass from the mother to the baby in the uterus, and allows waste to pass out from the baby to the mother
vagina	the passage into which the erect penis is pushed and through which the baby is born
testes	these two egg-shaped organs are held in a sac of skin outside the male body and make sperm

? CHECK YOURSELF QUESTIONS

Q1 What are the functions of the digestive system?

Q2 What are the functions of the circulatory system?

Q3 Match the beginnings of these sentences about the functions of human body organs with the correct endings:

Beginnings	Endings
a The stomach	1 pumps blood around the body.
b Arteries are blood vessels that	2 carry oxygen.
c White cells	3 carry blood at low pressure back to the heart.
d Veins are blood vessels that	4 kill bacteria and viruses.
e The heart is a muscular organ that	5 starts the breakdown of protein.
f Red cells	6 completes the digestion of food and absorbs it into the bloodstream.
g The small intestine	7 carry blood at high pressure away from the heart.

What you should already know

- Plants have organs that enable processes such as reproduction to take place.
- The names and positions of the main organs in plants.

QUICK CHECK!

These drawings show parts of a flower after they have been dissected from the plant. What are the names of each part?

1

a

b

c

2

3

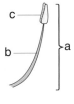

c

b

a

WHAT YOU NEED TO KNOW

- You saw in Revision Session 4 how different organs and organ systems in humans have different functions (jobs). This is also true for plants.

- The leaf is a plant organ. Its function is to use light to convert carbon dioxide and water into **biomass** (biological mass) by photosynthesis. The leaf also allows gas exchange of carbon dioxide and oxygen between the inside of the leaf and the atmosphere. We will look more closely at the leaf and how it is well suited to its job when we look at photosynthesis in Unit 2.

- The root is an organ specialised to take up water and minerals into the plant and to help anchor the plant into the soil.

- The flower is an **organ system** made up of male and female sex organs. The function of the flower is to enable the plant to reproduce sexually, i.e. to make seeds so that new young plants will be produced.

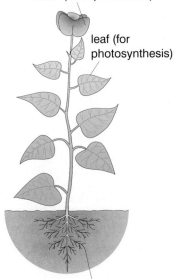

flower (for reproduction)

leaf (for photosynthesis)

roots (for anchoring and absorbing water and minerals)

Answers
1 a stigma b style   c ovary
2 petal
3 a stamen b filament   c anther

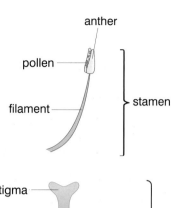

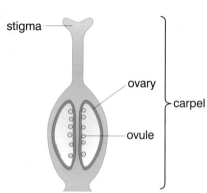

THE FUNCTION OF THE FLOWER

- The function of the flower is to bring about reproduction. This ensures that there are plenty of young plants that may survive when the parent plant dies. You have learned the names of plant parts. Now we are going to consider the function of each part of the flower.

- Flowering plants reproduce **sexually**. This means that the first cell of the new plant is made by a male sex cell joining with a female sex cell. This joining together of sex cells is called **fertilisation**.

- The male and female parts are specialised for reproduction. It is the job of the male parts to make the male sex cell. The male sex cell is called a pollen grain.

- It is the job of the female parts to make the female sex cell. The female sex cell is an ovule.

- The male and female sex cells are called **gametes**. Flowers normally use the wind or insects to make sure that these two sex cells are brought together so that fertilisation can take place. The table lists the male and female parts of a flower with their function.

Male part	Function
anther	makes the pollen
filament	supports the anther
pollen	the male sex cell (gamete) which fertilises the female sex cell (ovule)

Female part	Function
stigma	receives the pollen (it is sticky to make sure the pollen stays there)
ovary	makes the ovules and provides a place for seeds to develop, grows into a fruit after fertilisation
ovule	the female sex cell (gamete) which is fertilised by the male sex cell

- The anther and filament together are called the **stamen**. The stigma, ovary and ovule together are called the **carpel**.

- Pollen must travel from the anther (where it is made) to the stigma. This is called **pollination**. In some types of flower, insects pollinate the flower. If insects are needed to pollinate a flower, the flower usually has brightly coloured petals and a strong scent to attract them.

- Wind-pollinated flowers usually have smaller, less brightly coloured petals but have their anthers hanging out to allow the pollen to be spread by the wind. Usually, the stigma of a wind-pollinated flower also hangs out from the flower to help catch any pollen being carried by the air. The stigma of some plants looks like a feathery net to make it better for catching pollen.

THE FUNCTION OF THE ROOT

- The root (see right) secures or anchors the plant into the soil. Its other function is to take up water and minerals from the soil. For the root to be as efficient as possible, it has a very large surface area. This is produced by the main roots having smaller roots branching off them. These smaller roots are also branched to make the surface area as large as possible. The finest roots are actually single cells called **root hairs**.

? CHECK YOURSELF QUESTIONS

Q1 Write down one function of the leaf.

Q2 What is the function of the flower?

Q3 What are the functions of the root?

Q4 Explain what each of the following parts of a flower does to help bring about successful reproduction:

    stigma
    petal
    ovary
    ovule
    anther
    pollen

The Properties of Metals

What you should already know

- Different materials have different properties.

- Different materials have different uses because of their particular properties.

- There are three states of matter: solid, liquid and gas.

QUICK CHECK!

Solve these six clues to build the stack of words. Identify the letter which all the words have in common.

1	**A**			
2	**I**			
3	**H**			
4	**R**			
5	**S**			
6		**E**		

1 Metal container for fizzy drinks.
2 A circle of metal or the sound from a bicycle bell.
3 Metal will do this when it is brightly polished.
4 A bouncy coil of metal.
5 This happens to iron when it is left out in the rain.
6 A compass needle points north because it is _____ .

WHAT YOU NEED TO KNOW

- Metals are a very important group of substances and they have many properties in common. All metals are shiny if they are pure (especially if they are polished). Many of them are a silvery colour, but copper and gold are not. Colour and lustre (shine) are probably the first properties you would use to decide if something was metallic.

- All metals are solid at 20°C with one exception. Mercury is a liquid at this temperature.

WHY METALS ARE USEFUL

- Metals have been used throughout history for making tools and household objects such as pots and pans. This is because metals are generally very strong and can withstand heat (they have high melting points). Another useful property is that it is fairly easy to change their shape. They can be drawn out into wires or tubes, or flattened into sheets and they still keep their strength.

- There are some other important properties that you cannot see but you can still test for. The most important one is conductivity. All metals are excellent conductors of both thermal energy and electricity and both of these properties can be put to good use.

Answers:
1 CAN   2 RING   3 SHINE
4 SPRING   5 RUSTING
6 MAGNETIC
The common letter is N

The property of conducting thermal energy is called **thermal conductivity**. It is useful in cooking pans because it allows thermal energy to pass through the metal in order to heat the food inside.

- All metals allow electricity to pass through them. This property is called **electrical conductivity** and it can be demonstrated using the apparatus shown.

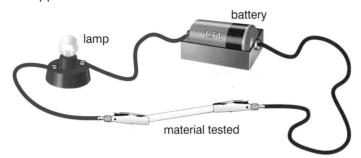

- The material to be tested is placed between two crocodile clips to complete a circuit. If the bulb lights up, the electricity is passing round the circuit and through the material, so it must be a conductor. The table shows the results of this test for four different materials.

Material	Does lamp light?	Conductor
copper	yes	✓
wood	no	✗
steel	yes	✓
rubber	no	✗

- A few metals are magnetic. The most important is iron, but nickel and cobalt are also magnetic. Another magnetic substance is steel, which is an **alloy** containing iron.

- An alloy is a mixture of different metals or a mixture of a metal and non-metals. Brass is a mixture of copper and tin; pewter is a mixture of tin and lead; steel is an alloy of iron which is made by adding small quantities of carbon (a non-metal).

- All alloys have the properties of metals and they are made to produce a metallic substance which is suitable for a particular purpose.

PROPERTIES OF NON-METALS
- Metals have many properties in common, but non-metals are much more varied in their properties. The appearance of non-metals tends to be dull (not shiny), their colours are varied and many non-metals exist as liquids or gases at room temperature.

- Non-metals that are solid at room temperature tend to be brittle rather than flexible. Some of them occur as powders and they are generally not very strong. They do not conduct thermal energy or electricity well, and are therefore thermal and electrical insulators.

- One exception to the pattern of properties for non-metals is carbon. Two different forms of carbon are diamond and graphite. Diamond is very hard and graphite fibres, used in sporting equipment, are very strong. Graphite will conduct electricity well. These are not typical properties of non-metals.

- You need to be able to classify substances as metals or non-metals. The table gives a summary of the most common properties of most metals and most non-metals. There are some exceptions in each group which have some of these properties but do not have some of the others.

Metals	Non-metals
good conductor of electricity	poor conductor of electricity
good thermal conductor	poor thermal conductor
shiny	dull
usually silvery	different colours
usually high melting point	usually low melting point
flexible	brittle
usually strong	usually weak

? CHECK YOURSELF QUESTIONS

Q1 Describe how you could test if a material conducts electricity. Use a diagram if that is helpful.

Q2 Summarise the most common properties of both metals and non-metals.

Q3 a For this table of data decide whether the substances are metals or non-metals.

b Which one of the non-metals shows some unusual properties?

Substance	Conducts electricity	Conducts thermal energy	Colour	Flexibility	Approximate melting point	Strength	Metal?
1	✓	✓	silvery	very flexible	medium	strong	
2	✓	✗	black	brittle	very high	strong	
3	✗	✗	yellow	brittle	low	weak	
4	✓	✓	brown	very flexible	high	strong	
5	✓	✓	grey	flexible	high	strong	
6	✗	✗	brown	brittle	low	weak	

> **What you should already know**
>
> • The scientific meanings of the terms 'evaporation' and 'condensation'.
>
> • The correct context in which to use each of these words to correctly describe each sort of change.
>
> • Different materials change state at different temperatures.

QUICK CHECK!

The photographs below show examples of evaporation or condensation. For each example, decide which one of these two changes is taking place?

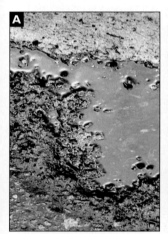

A puddle drying up on a sunny day

Droplets of water forming on a cold bottle

Clothes drying on a windy day

Water droplets forming on a cold window pane

WHAT YOU NEED TO KNOW

• When a liquid boils it changes to a gas. The temperature at which this happens is different for each type of liquid. The boiling temperature of water is 100°C, but liquid water can change to a gas at lower temperatures by the process of **evaporation**.

• At any temperature when water is liquid, there are always some water particles that move fast enough to escape from the surface of the liquid. The higher the temperature of the water, the more particles there are that are moving fast enough to escape from the surface of the water. This means that the rate of evaporation is faster at higher temperatures.

Answers:
Evaporation taking place in A and C
Condensation taking place in B and D

- The other two factors that affect the rate of evaporation from a liquid are:
  - the amount of water vapour present in the air immediately above the surface of the liquid;
  - the speed at which air is moving past the surface of the liquid.

- For any liquid – not just water – the rate of evaporation from its surface is greatest if the liquid is hot and the air immediately above it is dry and moving quickly. This is why wet clothes hanging on a washing line will dry quickly on a windy and sunny day.

- The water that evaporates from washing – along with the huge volume of water that evaporates from rivers, lakes and seas – rises into the air. As it rises, it cools and turns back to water as tiny droplets which form clouds. These droplets get larger and larger until they eventually fall as rain.

- The process by which gases, including water vapour, turn into liquids is called **condensation**. This process is the opposite of evaporation. The diagram below summarises the reversible change from liquid to gas which is happening constantly all around us.

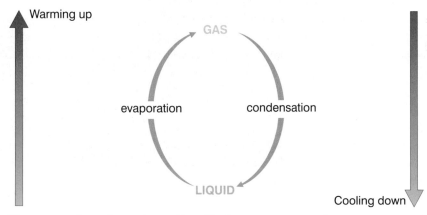

- The examples of condensation that we see around us occur because water vapour comes into contact with much cooler air or a cold surface. Once in contact, the water vapour loses thermal energy and cools to a temperature where it changes from gas to liquid. What we often call 'condensation' appears on a cold mirror in a 'steamy' bathroom. What appears on the mirror is actually water that has been formed by the process of condensation.

- Anything left to 'dry' does so by losing liquid by evaporation. Evaporation is used to good effect in applying paint. Paint is a mixture of coloured particles and a liquid. When it is applied to a wall or ceiling, the paint comes into contact with warm air and the liquid evaporates. This leaves a solid coat of paint on the wall.

- Inside its sealed container, the paint remains fluid because the liquid is prevented from evaporating by the air-tight lid. However, if the paint tin is left for several days with the lid removed, the paint at the surface will lose its liquid by evaporation and form a thick solid 'skin' on top of the remaining liquid paint.

- On a rainy day you and your classmates may have slightly damp clothing when you go into your classroom. Very soon the windows may 'steam up' (become covered with condensed water). Because the room is warm, water can evaporate from your clothing into the air. The water vapour in the air then condenses on the windows which are colder than the rest of the room.

? CHECK YOURSELF QUESTIONS

Q1 Which change of state occurs when evaporation takes place?

Q2 Which change of state occurs when condensation takes place?

Q3 What three factors affect the rate of evaporation of water from clothes hanging on a washing line?

Q4 Why does liquid paint 'dry out' when the lid is left off?

Q5 What is the name of the liquid that is often called 'condensation'?

Elements, Compounds and Mixtures

What you should already know

- All matter is made of particles.

- There is a huge range of different substances both naturally occurring and man-made.

QUICK CHECK!

Write the answers to these questions in the grid below. This will then spell out, reading top to bottom, the word for a substance made of only one kind of atom.

1. This compound is needed by all living things.
2. This metal element is very precious.
3. This element is given out by plants during photosynthesis.
4. Elements that can conduct electricity are generally these.
5. This element makes up most of the air around us.
6. This metal element is essential in our diet.
7. The smallest particles of matter.

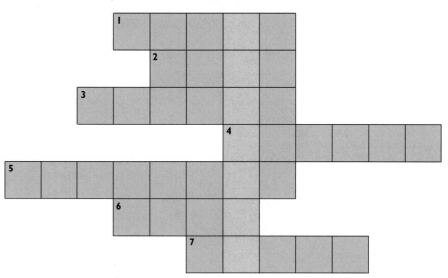

WHAT YOU NEED TO KNOW

- All substances are made up of the naturally occuring **elements** in the periodic table (see page 108).

- These elements can all exist on their own, or combine together by **chemical reactions** to form **compounds**. Elements and compounds can also exist together as **mixtures**. Where elements, and/or compounds, are in a mixture there has been **no** chemical reaction and it is easy to separate the elements or compounds from each other.

Answers
1 WATER 2 GOLD 3 OXYGEN
4 METALS 5 NITROGEN 6 IRON
7 ATOMS

- Think of sea water. Sea water is a mixture of two compounds, water and salt (sodium chloride). The water is a compound of hydrogen and oxygen. The salt is also a compound, of sodium and chlorine. It is quite easy to separate the salt from the water as there has been no chemical reaction – but to get the sodium from the salt or the oxygen from the water would be very difficult because there has been a chemical reaction to form the compound.

Salt   Sodium   Chlorine

- When elements form a compound they can change their nature completely. Water is made up from a chemical reaction between two gases – hydrogen and oxygen. Salt is made from a reaction between sodium which is a metal that burns when it is in contact with water, and chlorine which is a green, poisonous gas.

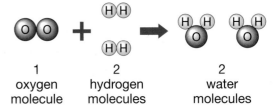

1	2	2
oxygen molecule	hydrogen molecules	water molecules

CHECK YOURSELF QUESTIONS

Q1 Separate these substances into elements, mixtures and compounds.

Water

Air

Oxygen

Salt

Iron oxide

Hydrogen

Copper

Nitrogen

Tin

Brass

Q1 Which of these diagrams shows:

a) a pure element

b) a mixture of elements

c) a mixture of compounds

d) a mixture of one compound and two elements.

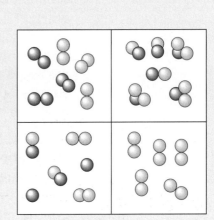

REVISION SESSION 9 — Separating Mixtures

What you should already know

- Mixtures of substances can be separated.

- What happens during the processes of evaporation and condensation.

- The four most common methods of separating mixtures are evaporation, filtration, distillation and chromatography.

- How to describe some of the methods used to separate simple mixtures.

QUICK CHECK!

Read the clues below and write your answers in the space provided. To help you, some of the letters have been filled in. Then put together the highlighted letters to reveal a hidden word reading the letters from top to bottom.

Because sugar can dissolve, we say it is
A puddle dries up because the water
Different dyes can be separated using
It's a lot easier with a funnel:
If you cool water enough it will
Process used in making whisky:
Leave ice cream in the sun and it will
Sand won't dissolve. It is
When a gas turns to a liquid it
A liquid which will dissolve a solid is a

The hidden word is

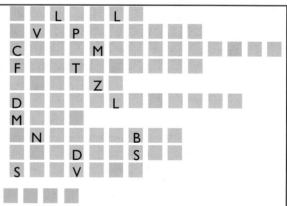

WHAT YOU NEED TO KNOW

- Different materials have different properties. For example, different liquids have different **boiling points**. Different solids may be soluble or insoluble in a particular **solvent**. Separation methods work because they take advantage of the different properties of the materials in a mixture – each material behaves differently. The four main methods of separating mixtures are described briefly here.

EVAPORATION

- **Evaporation** is used to separate soluble solids from their solvent. The solvent evaporates leaving the solid behind in the container. This can be achieved either by heating the **solution** in an evaporating dish or by leaving for a few days in a warm place.

Answers
SOLUBLE EVAPORATES
CHROMATOGRAPHY
FILTRATION FREEZE
DISTILLATION MELT
INSOLUBLE CONDENSES
SOLVENT
The missing word is
SEPARATION.

FILTRATION

- You need to know that some substances are soluble and that others are insoluble in water. It is a good idea to learn some of the more common ones. For example, salt, copper sulphate and sugar are soluble in water; sand, mud and chalk are insoluble. **Filtration** is used to separate insoluble substances from liquids. This works because an insoluble substance such as sand has particles that are too big to pass between the fibres of the filter paper. The liquid part of the mixture passes through the filter. The insoluble part is stopped by the filter paper.

DISTILLATION

- **Distillation** is used to separate a mixture of liquids. The mixture is heated in a closed container until one liquid boils. You collect the vapour and cool it. It condenses to form the pure liquid. You can also use this method to separate liquid from a mixture of liquid and solid.

CHROMATOGRAPHY

- **Chromatography** is used to separate different coloured dyes. The dyes which are more soluble move further up the chromatography paper. The dyes move different distances before they can no longer remain in solution, so they separate from each other.

CHOOSING A METHOD

- When you have to suggest a method of separation for a mixture, you need to think carefully about the states and properties of the substances in the mixture. A useful way to decide which method to use is a checklist like this one.

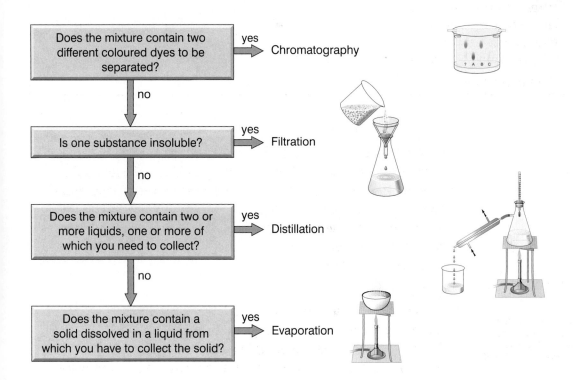

```
Does the mixture contain two          yes
different coloured dyes to be      ──────►  Chromatography
separated?
        │ no
        ▼
Is one substance insoluble?           yes
                                   ──────►  Filtration
        │ no
        ▼
Does the mixture contain two or       yes
more liquids, one or more of       ──────►  Distillation
which you need to collect?
        │ no
        ▼
Does the mixture contain a            yes
solid dissolved in a liquid from   ──────►  Evaporation
which you have to collect the solid?
```

Q1 Sand is insoluble in water and copper sulphate is soluble.

a What will happen if a mixture of these two substances is stirred into water?

b What happens if you then pour this mixture through a filter paper.

c How could you recover the copper sulphate from the mixture?

Q2 How can you separate pure water from a solution of salt and water?

Q3 How can you separate a mixture of different oils? They are all liquid and have different boiling points.

Q4 Why is evaporation not suitable for collecting water from sea water?

Q5 Shanti has used red, blue and yellow dyes to make three new colours:
blue and yellow were mixed to produce green;
blue and red were mixed to produce purple;
red and yellow were mixed to produce orange.

Now she wants to separate them using chromatography. She has set up the apparatus shown to carry out this experiment. She knows that the yellow dye travels furthest up the paper and that the blue dye travels the least distance. Draw a diagram to show what the filter paper would look like when the experiment is finished.

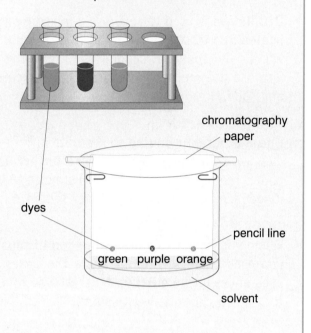

What you should already know

- Light travels from a source.
- Light cannot pass through some materials, leading to the formation of a shadow.
- Light is reflected by shiny surfaces.
- Light travels in straight lines.

QUICK CHECK!

Try to find seven words to do with reflection in the wordsearch. When you have found the words, use them to fill in the blanks in the sentence alongside the wordsearch.

R	E	F	L	E	C	T
O	P	R	I	Y	G	L
R	L	E	G	A	M	I
R	A	S	H	I	N	Y
I	N	Y	T	V	I	S
M	E	X	S	P	O	J

A M _ _ _ _ _ has a

S _ _ _ _, P _ _ _ _

surface that is able to

R _ _ _ _ _ _ R _ _ _

of L _ _ _ _ to form

an I _ _ _ _.

WHAT YOU NEED TO KNOW

- You can read the writing on this page because light from the sun or a lamp is shining onto the page. Because the surface of the paper is uneven, light that hits the paper is scattered (spread out in all directions) and some of this light reaches your eyes.

- Light has to enter your eyes before you are able to see the paper and other objects. All objects that are not luminous can only be seen because they scatter light that falls onto them. Light is not reflected in a regular way unless the surface it hits is shiny, such as a mirror, polished metal or very calm water.

The words to find are:
MIRROR SHINY
PLANE REFLECT
RAYS LIGHT IMAGE.

Very calm sea water can reflect light like a mirror

- When a ray of light hits a plane (flat) mirror it is reflected. The diagram shows that the angle at which it hits the mirror (*i*) is the same as the angle at which it leaves the mirror (*r*).

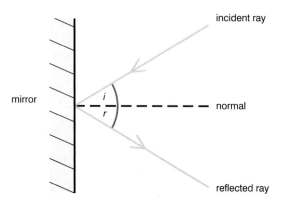

- The ray of light hitting the mirror is called the **incident ray** and the ray of light leaving the mirror is called the **reflected ray**. The dotted line is called the **normal**. This is a line drawn at right angles to the surface of the mirror where the ray of light hits it.

- Angle *i* is called the **angle of incidence** and angle *r* is called the **angle of reflection**. These two angles are always the same size for the reflection of light at a plane mirror. We can write this as:

  angle of incidence = angle of reflection
  i = *r*

- When you look at an object in the mirror, its image (what you see) appears to be:
  - the same size as the object;
  - the same distance behind the mirror as it is in front of the mirror;
  - the other way round (**laterally inverted**).

- The image is **virtual** – it is not really there, since you cannot catch it on a screen. These are the properties of any image seen in a mirror, including yourself, and you should try to remember them.

CHECK YOURSELF QUESTIONS

Q1 When light hits a plane mirror it is reflected. Which two diagrams correctly show how two different rays of light are reflected?

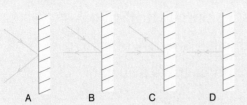

A B C D

Q2

Alex uses a periscope to look over a wall.

Copy and complete the diagram to show a ray of light coming from the tree to Alex's eye.

Alex can only see one creature in the tree; which one will he see?

Q3

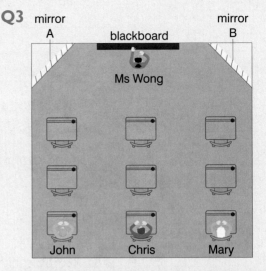

mirror A   blackboard   mirror B

Ms Wong

John   Chris   Mary

The pupils in Ms Wong's class think that she has 'eyes in the back of her head'. When she is writing on the blackboard she can still see which pupils are not working.

a How can she see the pupils when she is writing on the board?

b Complete the diagram with a ray of light to show how Ms Wong can see:
i John;
ii Mary.

c Ms Wong cannot see Chris. What should she do so that she can see him when she is writing on the blackboard?

> **What you should already know**
>
> • Sound is produced when an object vibrates.
>
> • You cannot always see the object vibrating.
>
> • Sound can travel through a variety of materials.
>
> • Sound cannot travel through a vacuum.

QUICK CHECK!

Fill in the table to say what is vibrating and causing the sound produced by each of the musicians.

Object	What vibrates?
Drum	
Guitar	
Saxophone	
Tambourine	
Singer	

Answers:
DRUM SKIN   STRINGS   REED
METAL DISCS
VOCAL CHORDS

WHAT YOU NEED TO KNOW

- We can hear a wide range of different sounds. These sounds vary in two important ways. They can have a different **loudness** and a different **pitch**. If you are playing a piano, you can vary the loudness of a note by hitting that key harder. You can vary the pitch of the sound by pressing keys that hit different strings.

- When we talk about sounds, we discuss sound **waves**. Sound waves are invisible. The only way we can 'see' them is to use an **oscilloscope**. An oscilloscope is similar to a television. It displays electrical signals as lines on its screen.

- A microphone can be connected to an oscilloscope so that when a sound is made a trace is seen on the screen. This trace represents the sound wave.

- The height of the wave is called the **amplitude**. It tells us how loud the sound is. The larger the amplitude of the vibration, the louder the sound.

- The length of a single wave is called the **wavelength**. This is the distance from one point on one wave to the same point on the next wave. A wave with a short wavelength represents a high pitch sound. If the wavelength is long then the pitch of the sound is low.

- If an object is vibrating very quickly (very frequently) there are more waves on the screen, so their wavelength is shorter. The pitch of the note will be higher and we say it has a higher **frequency**. If the object is vibrating slowly (not very frequently) then there are few waves on the screen, and the wavelength of the waves is longer. The pitch will be lower because it has a lower frequency.

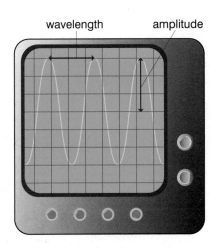

wavelength   amplitude

loud sound
high frequency

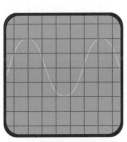

loud sound
low frequency

quiet sound
high frequency

quiet sound
low frequency

CHANGING THE LOUDNESS OF A SOUND

- The loudness of a sound can be increased by increasing the size of the vibrations that are providing the sound. You might pluck a guitar string harder or hit a drum skin harder to increase the loudness of a sound. Reducing the size of the vibrations producing the sound will make the sound quieter.

CHANGING THE PITCH OF A SOUND

- To alter the pitch of a sound produced by a vibrating object you have to change the size of the vibrating object. Look at the two musical instruments on the left.

- On an organ, the low pitched notes are produced by air vibrating in the long pipes and the high notes are produced by air vibrating in the short pipes.

- On a xylophone, the low pitched notes are produced by hitting the long bars and the high pitched notes are produced by the short bars.

? CHECK YOURSELF QUESTIONS

Q1

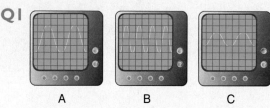

A   B   C

Three different sounds are represented by waves on the oscilloscope screens above.

a Which wave shows the sound with the highest pitch?

b Which wave shows the quietest sound?

c Which two sounds have the same pitch?

d Which two sounds have the same amplitude?

e Which sound has the highest frequency?

Q2 Jim whistles into a microphone and the sound is displayed on an oscilloscope screen as shown in the diagram below. Tony then whistles into the microphone. Tony's whistle is twice as loud, and half of the pitch of Jim's.

a Complete the diagram to show what Tony's whistle would look like on the oscilloscope screen.

b Whose whistle has the greater frequency?

What you should already know

- The apparent position of the Sun changes over the course of a day.
- The Earth revolves once every twenty-four hours.
- The Earth completes one orbit of the Sun every year.

QUICK CHECK!

Imagine someone from deepest space wanted to send a letter to you. Write your name and the full address that they would need to use on the envelope below.

name: _____

street: _____

town/city: _____

county: _____

country: _____

planet: _____

nearest star: _____

galaxy: _____

WHAT YOU NEED TO KNOW

- Every day the Sun appears to rise in the east and set in the west. People used to think that the Sun travelled around the Earth, but we now know that this is wrong. The Earth actually **orbits** the Sun. As it does this, it also spins round. It does one full turn in 24 hours. The Sun appears to move from east to west so the Earth must spin from west to east.

SUN

EARTH

North pole

South pole

Your address should end with Earth, Sun, Milky Way.

- The half of the Earth that faces the Sun is in daylight and the half of the Earth that is facing away from the Sun is in darkness. You can see from the diagram that the axis of the Earth (the line around which the Earth rotates) is tilted.

- When the Earth is in the position shown, the South Pole will have constant daylight and the North Pole will be in darkness. The northern hemisphere (half of the Earth) is tilting away from the Sun and the southern hemisphere is tilting towards the Sun. This happens in winter and causes our cold winters with short days and long nights.

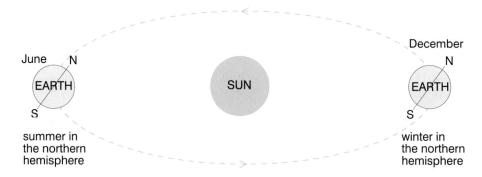

- In summer, however, the northern hemisphere is tilting towards the Sun. We have longer periods of daylight and shorter periods of darkness each day and the weather is warmer. It takes about 365 days (one year) for the Earth to make one complete orbit of the Sun.

- The Earth revolves on its axis, which makes the Sun appear to move across the sky each day. During the course of a year, the apparent path of the Sun across the sky changes.

- In this country, the apparent path taken by the Sun across the sky in December is lower than the path it appears to take in March and this is lower than the path the Sun appears to take in June. This change is because the northern hemisphere inclines (leans) towards the Sun in June and away from the Sun in December. During the winter months, the Sun appears to reach its highest point at 12.00 noon. During British Summer Time, when the clocks have gone forward by one hour, its highest point occurs at 1 p.m.

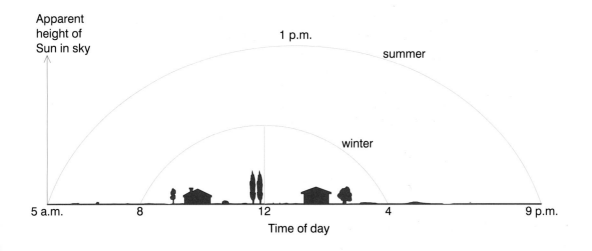

Apparent height of Sun in sky

1 p.m.

summer

winter

5 a.m.   8   12   4   9 p.m.

Time of day

CHECK YOURSELF QUESTIONS

Q1

North pole

EARTH

South pole

a Draw an arrow to show which way the Earth turns.

b Shade in the part of the Earth where it is dark.

c Is it day or night at the North Pole?

Q2 The diagram shows the path taken as the Earth orbits the Sun.

N
A
S

SUN

N
B
S

a How long does it take for the Earth to complete one orbit of the Sun?

b How long does it take for the Earth to turn once about its axis?

c What season is the southern hemisphere having when the Earth is in positions A and B?

REVISION SESSION 13 Electrical Circuits

> **What you should already know**
> - **Electricity can only flow when there is a complete circuit.**
> - **Metals are generally good conductors of electricity.**

QUICK CHECK!

Use your knowledge about electrical circuits to complete the grid below. Once you have completed it, one of the columns spells the name of a special kind of circuit.

1. For electricity to flow a circuit must be ....
2. The unit of electric current is the ....
3. Materials that allow electric current to flow are called ....
4. We measure current with an ....
5. These materials are good conductors of electricity ....
6. Materials that do not allow electric current to flow are called ....
7. Electricity is a means of transferring ....
8. The tiny particles that move around an electrical circuit are called ....

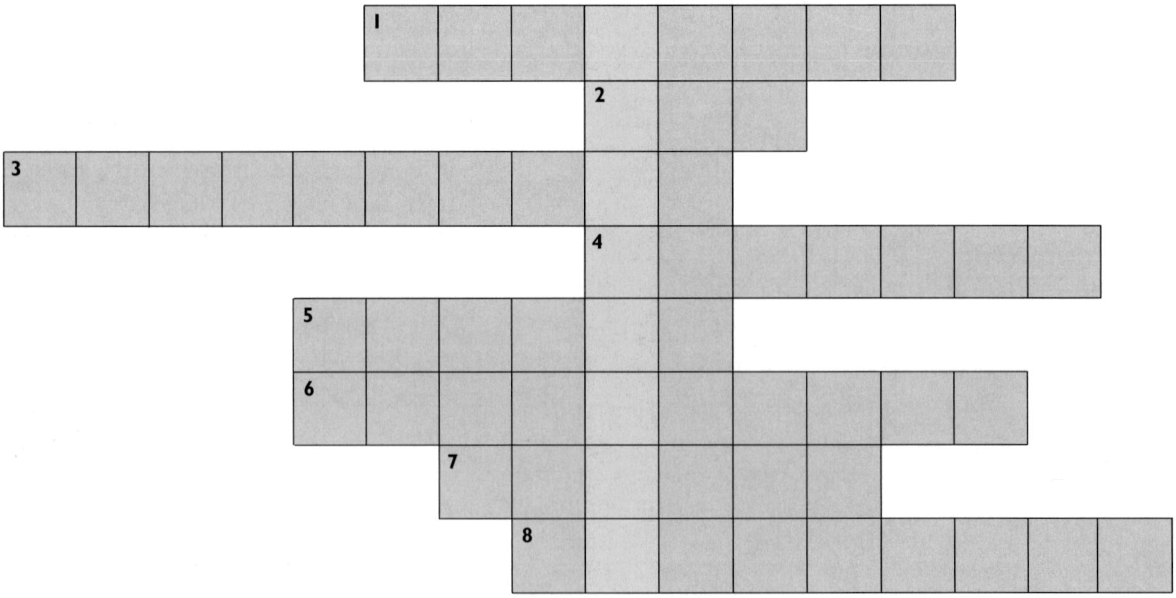

WHAT YOU NEED TO KNOW

- For electricity to flow there must be a complete circuit – but complete circuits can be arranged in different ways.
- In a **series circuit**, all the components are placed one after the other so that the electric current flows through each in turn. In a **parallel circuit**, the current divides and goes through several branches at once.

1.COMPLETE
2.AMP
3.CONDUCTORS
4.AMMETER
5.METALS
6.INSULATORS
7.ENERGY
8.ELECTRONS

- Remember that we always draw electrical circuits using **symbols** to represent the components.

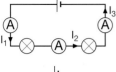

Wherever you measure the current in a **series circuit** it will always be the same. In this diagram all the ammeters will have the same reading.

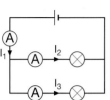

In a **parallel** circuit like this the current splits into the different branches. In this diagram the total of the readings in the two branches will add up to the same amount of current as that shown in the first ammeter.

Think of a string of Christmas tree lights:

- If they are connected in series, when you add more bulbs to a series circuit then all the bulbs will become less bright. If one bulb in a series circuit breaks then all the bulbs will go out.

- If the lights are connected in parallel then adding more bulbs will not make each individual bulb less bright and if one bulb goes out then the others will continue to work.

CHECK YOURSELF QUESTIONS

Q1 Identify these circuit symbols:

a) _____   b) _____   c _____

Q2 Look at these two circuits. If a bulb breaks in each of them what will happen?

If bulb A breaks bulb B will ....

....

If bulb B breaks then bulb A will ....
and bulb C will ....

1   Each of the animals in the drawings below belongs to a different group.

a   On the line beneath each drawing, write the name of the group the animal belongs to. Choose names from the list below.

(4 marks)

amphibians   crustaceans   insects   mammals   molluscs   reptiles

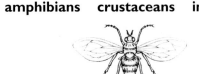

A _____   B _____

C _____   D _____

b   Which of the animals drawn above are invertebrates?
Give the correct letters.   *(2 marks)*

...............................and...................................   *maximum 6 marks*

2   Some pupils predicted that water will evaporate faster if the surrounding air temperature is higher.

To investigate their prediction they placed some water in containers in two different rooms.
a   Give **two** factors they should keep the same to make their investigation fair.

1. ....   *(1 mark)*

2. ....   *(1 mark)*

b   They recorded the mass of the water and the container in room 1 and room 2 every day for 5 days. The table below shows their results.

time (days)	mass of water and container (g)	
	room 1	room 2
0	100	100
1	92	85
2	80	72
3	72	54
4	60	45
5	46	30

The data shown in their table is **not** sufficient to test their prediction.
Explain why.

....

.... *(1 mark)*

They plotted their data for room 2 and
attempted to draw a line of best fit.

c Describe the mistake they made in
drawing the line of best fit.

....

....

....

....

....

(1 mark)

mass of
water and
container
(g)

d Using the data in the table plot the points for room 1.   *(1 mark)*

e Draw a line of best fit of the points you have drawn.   *(1 mark)*

f In which room did the water evaporate more quickly? Tick **one** box.

room 1 ☐   room 2 ☐

Use their data to explain your answer.

....

....
                                                                (1 mark)
                                        maximum 7 marks

3 The diagram shows an oak tree.

a An oak tree takes in water and oxygen from the soil.
Name **one** other **type** of substance an oak tree needs
to take in from the soil.

....

(1 mark)

b The roots of an oak tree are long and split into many smaller roots.
How does this help the tree to absorb water?

.... *(1 mark)*

c By the time winter comes, the oak tree has lost its leaves.
Explain why this stops the growth of an oak tree.

.... *(1 mark)*

d The drawing shows a caterpillar of a moth called the Oak Beauty.
These caterpillars feed on oak leaves and woodland birds eat them.

Describe how the appearance of the caterpillar can help it to survive.

.... —caterpillar

....

....

....

(2 marks)

maximum 5 marks

——— twig

4 Gold, iron and magnesium are elements which conduct electricity.

Sulphur and phosphorus are elements which do **not** conduct electricity.

When iron and sulphur are heated together, they react to form a new substance called iron sulphide.

a From the substances above, give:

(i) the name of a metal.. *(1 mark)*

(ii) the name of an element which is a non-metal

.... *(1 mark)*

(iii) the name of an element which will rust

.... *(1 mark)*

(iv) the name of a compound... *(1 mark)*

b When magnesium and sulphur are heated together, they react.
Write the name of the compound which is formed when magnesium reacts with sulphur.

.... *(1 mark)*

maximum 5 marks

5 Gravy powder contains:
- a brown substance to make the gravy brown
- cornflour to make the gravy thick

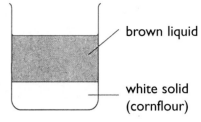
brown liquid

white solid (cornflour)

Dan mixed some gravy powder with cold water in a beaker.
An hour later, the contents of the beaker looked like this:

a Use the words in the list below to fill the gaps in the following sentences.

solvent   **solution**   **soluble**   **insoluble**

The brown substance dissolves in water to form a brown ....

The cornflour settles at the bottom of the beaker because it is .... in water.

Water is the .... in this experiment. *(3 marks)*

b Dan wanted to separate the brown liquid from the white solid.
What could he do to separate them?

.... *(1 mark)*

c Dan put a little of the brown liquid in a dish. The next day there was only a brown solid left in the dish. What had happened to the water?

....

.... *(1 mark)*

d Dan wanted to get pure water from the rest of the brown liquid.
He set up the apparatus shown here.

thermometer

water out

drops of pure water

Water vapour from the brown liquid changed into drops of pure water which were collected in the beaker. What process caused the drops of water to form from the vapour?

water vapour

brown liquid

heat

water in

Tick the correct box.

boiling ☐   condensing ☐   dissolving ☐   melting ☐   *(1 mark)*

maximum 6 marks

6 Sarah and Jim investigated the effect of temperature on the solubility of copper sulphate.

They dissolved copper sulphate crystals in the same volume of water until **no** more would dissolve. This means the solution was saturated. They measured the mass of copper sulphate needed to make a saturated solution using water at different temperatures.

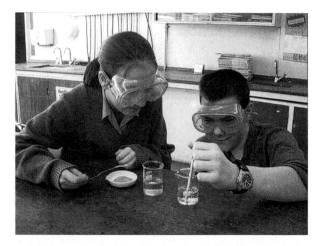

They plotted their results on a grid.

mass of dissolved copper sulphate crystals, in g

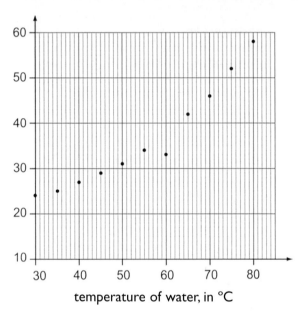

temperature of water, in °C

a (i) One of the mass readings appears to be wrong (anomalous). Circle the anomalous result on the graph. *(1 mark)*

    (ii) Draw a smooth curve of best fit on the graph. *(1 mark)*

    (ii) Use the graph to predict a more likely measurement of mass for the anomalous result.

                        .... g *(1 mark)*

b Suggest **one** mistake Sarah and Jim might have made to produce this anomalous result.

....

.... *(1 mark)*

maximum 4 marks

7 Lorna built the circuit drawn here.
All the bulbs are identical.

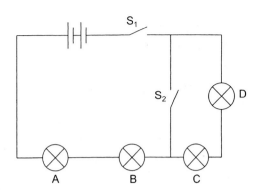

a Complete the table below by writing
on or **off** for each bulb.
One has been done for you.

switch		bulb			
S$_1$	S$_2$	A	B	C	D
open	open	off	off	off	off
open	closed				
closed	open				
closed	closed				

(1 mark)
(1 mark)
(1 mark)

b Lorna then built a different circuit
as shown here.
How could Lorna get both bulbs to light
at the same time in this circuit?

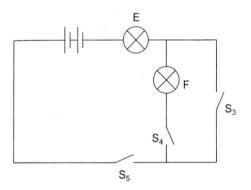

....

....

....

....

(1 mark)

maximum 4 marks

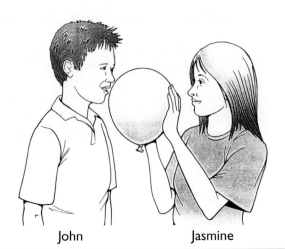

8 Jasmine is deaf. She blows up a balloon
and holds it near to John's mouth.
She cannot hear John's voice, but she
can tell that he is speaking by feeling
the balloon.

John   Jasmine

a How can Jasmine tell that John is speaking by feeling the balloon?

....

.... *(1 mark)*

b John shouts loudly. How will the balloon feel different to Jasmine now?

....

.... *(1 mark)*

c Loudness is measured in decibels. The table below shows the loudness of some sounds.

sound	loudness, in decibels
whispering	20
normal talking	60
disco	100
road drill	120
space rocket taking off	190

Jasmine's balloon bursts. What would be the most likely range of loudness of
the sound produced when the balloon bursts? Tick the correct box. *(1 mark)*

below 60 decibels ☐   60-120 decibels ☐

120-190 decibels ☐   above 190 decibels ☐

d **(i)** Very loud sounds can damage a person's ears.
In what way can the ears be damaged?

.... *(1 mark)*

(ii) Some people work in very noisy places.
How can they protect their ears?

.... *(1 mark)*

maximum 5 marks

9 On 11th August 1999 there was an eclipse. The shadow of the Moon passed over part of the Earth.

a The diagram below shows the Moon, the Moon's shadow and the Earth.

On the diagram, draw an arrow pointing towards where the Sun must be.

(1 mark)

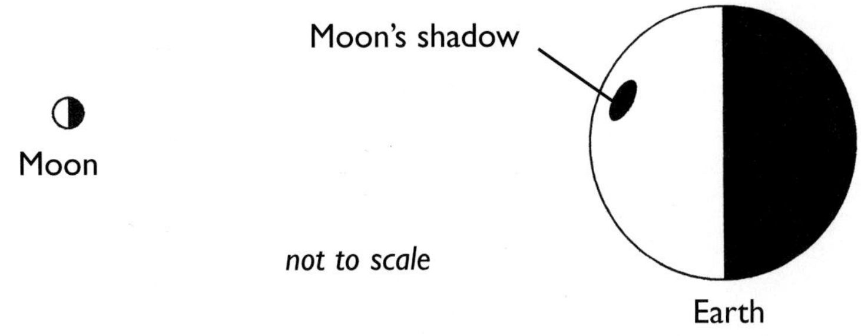

Moon

Moon's shadow

not to scale

Earth

b At about midday the Moon's shadow passed over Cornwall, in England. Where, in the sky, was the Sun at midday? Tick the correct box.

towards the North ☐   towards the East ☐

towards the West ☐   towards the South ☐   *(1 mark)*

c The map shows the shape of the Moon's shadow and the path it took across Cornwall.

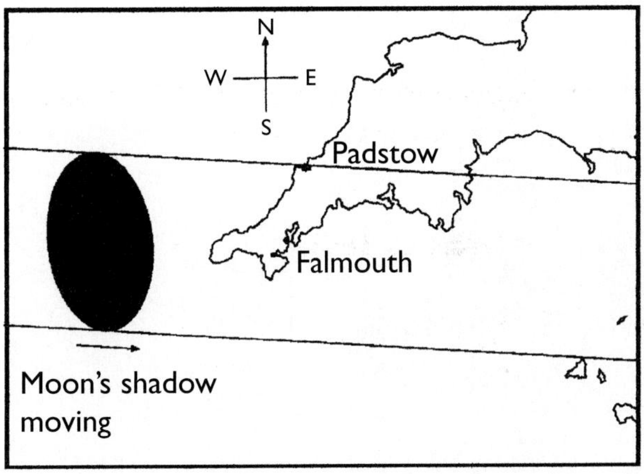

The Moon's shadow took about 2 minutes to move across a house in Falmouth.
It took less than 2 minutes to move across a house in Padstow.

Explain why it took less time for the Moon's shadow to move across a house in Padstow than to move across one in Falmouth.

N
W — E
S

Padstow

Falmouth

Moon's shadow moving

....

.... *(1 mark)*

d Why does the Moon's shadow move over the surface of the Earth?

....

.... *(1 mark)*

maximum 4 marks

total possible marks 46

total marks ☐

Scientific Enquiry – Ideas and Evidence

> **What you should already know**
> - Scientists carry out experiments to test their ideas.

WHAT YOU NEED TO KNOW

WHAT IS EVIDENCE?

- We can all have ideas and opinions on all sorts of things. Scientists must support the ideas that they have with evidence. Evidence comes from investigations, experiments and observations which scientists make to show that the ideas they are putting forward are correct.

- An opinion would be to say that winters seem to be less cold than they used to be. Evidence would be to use temperature measurements over a period of years to determine whether the annual mean temperature has risen by a number of degrees over a number of years.

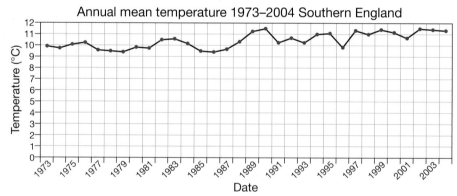

Annual mean temperature 1973–2004 Southern England

- It was an opinion that the earth was flat. The voyages of Christopher Columbus and Ferdinand Magellan provided evidence that the Earth is round.

- New evidence often comes along to show that an idea is wrong or not complete. That is really what science is – ideas that people test by experiment or observation to show that a previously held idea needs to be changed or developed in some way.

ASKING THE RIGHT QUESTION

- If you have an idea that you want to test by looking for evidence, you must be very sure what your experiment is going to show.

- You must ask the right question and select and control the right variables to be sure that you are really testing what you think you are testing so that you really have the evidence you want at the end! This can be especially difficult in experiments which involve people, animals or even plants where there can be lots of variables which can be hard to control or measure.

- For example, suppose you want to know whether increasing the mass of an object increases the friction between the object and the surface. To test this idea you must change the mass (this is your independent variable) and measure how much force it takes to overcome friction and make the object start to move (the dependent variable). You must control the surface the object is resting on, the surface area of the object and the way in which you take the measurements. The time it takes, the temperature of surface and the colour of the object are all variables that are not relevant to this enquiry.

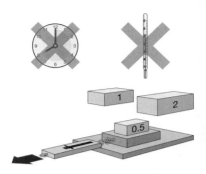

? CHECK YOURSELF QUESTIONS

Q1 a A group of pupils want to find out if boys have bigger feet than girls. They carry out a survey of all the pupils in their school. Which of the following pieces of information would NOT be of any value in this survey?

   (i)   Whether each person they ask is male or female
   (ii) How old they are
   (iii) How tall they are
   (iv) Their shoe size
   (v)   Their eye colour
   (vi) Their hair colour

b Why would asking everyone in the school make the survey better than just asking their own class.

Q2 Look at the table below. There is an enquiry, an independent variable, a dependent variable and a factor to be controlled. Decide if these are suitable for the enquiry and, if not, suggest a better one.

Enquiry	Independent variable	Dependent variable	Control variable
Whether exercise affects pulse rates	Amount of exercise	Pulse rate	Fitness of the people taking part
Which paper towel is the most absorbent	Different kinds of paper towel	Amount of water	Temperature of the water
Where woodlice most like to live	Conditions for woodlice to choose	How long it takes for the woodlice to make their choice	The size of the woodlice
What conditions are the best for growing broad bean plants	Amount of water	Height of bean plants	The size of the plant pot
What material is best for insulating cups of hot drinks	Temperature of the drinks	How long it takes for the liquid to reach room temperature	The size and shape of the containers

Variation

WHAT YOU NEED TO KNOW

• There are great differences between animals or plants of different species. For example, a lion and a common frog both belong to the vertebrate family but they are very different. Even within one species we find many differences between individual members. If we concentrate on our own species – human beings – we can see a great many differences between people. Look at the picture below and try to spot as many differences as you can between the people shown:

• The photograph shows that there is a lot of variety of individuals within each species. We say that a species shows **variation**. A survey was carried out looking at the height of all the 14-year-old pupils in a particular school. The results are shown in the bar chart that follows.

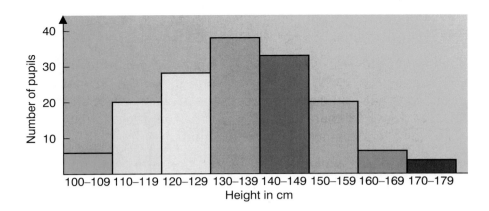

WHAT CAUSES MEMBERS OF A SPECIES TO BE SO DIFFERENT FROM ONE ANOTHER?

- There are two main causes of variation (differences) within a species: **inherited** causes and **environmental** causes.

INHERITED CAUSES

- Children look more or less like one or both of their parents. They inherit things from their parents, such as eye colour, hair colour, nose and ear shape. The plans for these inherited features are carried inside the nucleus of each cell on tiny thread-like structures called **chromosomes**. Each of us has inherited information from both of our parents. Half of this information comes from the father and half from the mother.

- A baby's life starts when a sperm from its father joins an egg from its mother. The nucleus of the sperm cell carries the father's half of the information and the nucleus of the egg cell carries the mother's half of the inherited information. At **fertilisation**, the sperm's nucleus joins with the egg cell's nucleus and the inherited make-up of the new baby is determined by the combination of information from the parents.

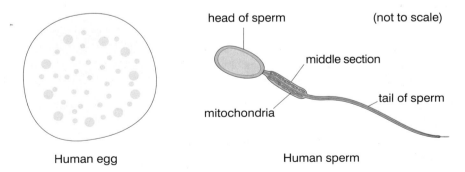

Human egg

Human sperm

ENVIRONMENTAL CAUSES

- The information that we inherit from our parents is not the only thing that decides our characteristics. Even if a child has two tall parents and inherits information that gives them the potential to be tall, they may still turn out to be quite short if they do not eat a good balanced diet.

- In a similar way, if they eat too much food they may become fat, despite what their inherited information may say.

- In other words, the way a child is brought up, what they eat, the education they receive and the amount of exercise they take, amongst many other influences, can all have an effect on the appearance and characteristics of the person. These influences are called environmental causes of variation.

- Scientists have studied sets of identical twins to try to find out more about the importance of inherited and environmental causes of variation. Identical twins have exactly the same inherited information, because they both grow from the same fertilised egg. Any differences between identical twins must be due to environmental influences.

CHECK YOURSELF QUESTIONS

Q1 Make a list of ten characteristics that vary between human beings.

Q2 Complete the sentences below using the words at the bottom of the page.

Children .... some features from their parents. For example, ... colour, ... colour and .... shape are all features that are passed on from parents to their children. Each child gets .... their inherited information from their .... and .... from their .... .The inherited information from the father is carried inside the .... and the mother's part of the information is carried in the .... .These two sets of information are brought together when the sperm .... with the egg. This is called ....

egg	eye	fertilisation
father	hair	half
inherit	mother	nose
joins	sperm	half

Q3 A list of variations that are found between humans is given below:

natural hair colour, eye colour, height, weight, nose shape, the accent you speak with, naturally curly hair, intelligence, blood group, the ability to roller-skate

Complete the table putting each variation into one column depending on whether you think it has an environmental cause, an inherited cause or if it is caused by both the environment and inherited information.

only the environment causes these:	inherited information causes these:	both the environment and inherited information causes these:

Cell Structure

> **What you should already know**
>
> - The main functions of some organs of the human body and of flowering plants.
> - How the functions of organs are essential to the organism (plant or animal).
> - Animals and plants are made up of cells.

WHAT YOU NEED TO KNOW

You need to be able to list the main features of plant and animal cells and be able to see the differences between them.

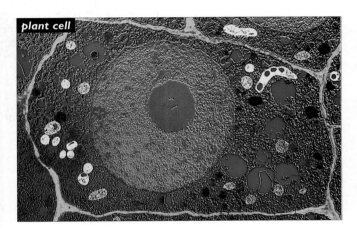
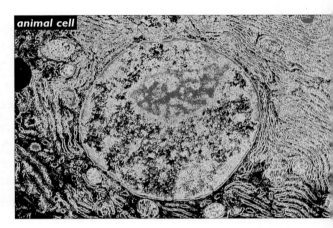

- If you look at animal or plant tissue under a microscope, you can see that the tissue is made up of lots of very tiny building blocks. Scientists call these tiny building blocks **cells**. Cells are too small to see without using a microscope to magnify them. All living organisms are made up of cells.

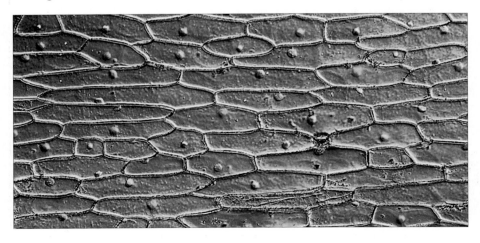

This magnified view of the epidermis of an onion shows the arrangement of its cells. The spot inside each cell is its nucleus.

A CLOSER LOOK AT CELLS

- If you turn up the magnification on your microscope, from low power to medium or high power, then you can see that the cells are made up of smaller parts. The top diagram shows the parts of a human cheek cell as seen through a high-power microscope.

- Each part of the cell has a reason for being there – a function that is essential to the working of the cell.

- The **nucleus** is the control centre of the cell. It contains information that determines which chemicals will be made and the structure of the cell. The nucleus contains chemical codes that control the development and function of the whole organism.

- The **cytoplasm** is a watery jelly-like liquid that fills the cell. Inside it, important chemical reactions take place and we find other cell parts such as the nucleus.

- The **cell membrane** is the outer layer of the cell. It allows some substances to pass in and out of the cell, e.g. carbon dioxide and oxygen. Other substances cannot pass through, e.g. protein molecules.

- The human cheek cell is a typical animal cell. However, not all animal cells are the same. Most have the parts we have listed, but some animal cells look very different to others. This is because each cell type has a special job to do. We will look more closely at these cell specialisations in Unit 3 Revision Session 3, *Specialised Cells* (pages 99-102).

PLANT CELLS

- Plant cells are different from animal cells in some important ways. Look closely at the diagram on the left, which shows a plant cell from a leaf. Study the parts of the plant cell carefully.

- Plant cells contain all of the parts also present in animal cells, but there are some other important structures.

cytoplasm   nucleus

cell membrane

Human cheek cell

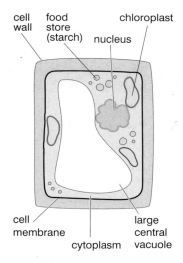

cell wall   food store (starch)   chloroplast

nucleus

cell membrane

cytoplasm   large central vacuole

Plant cell from a leaf

CELL PARTS FOUND IN ALL PLANT CELLS

- The **cell wall** is the outermost covering of the plant cell. It is made of a substance called **cellulose**. Fibre in our diet is cellulose from plant cells. The cell wall is relatively strong and tough and gives the cell its shape.

- A large **vacuole** contains a solution of sugars and salts that we call **cell sap**. The vacuole is in the middle of the cell and it takes up most of the volume of the cell. This is not true of animal cells, which may have small, temporary vacuoles.

CELL PARTS FOUND IN MANY PLANT CELLS

- **Chloroplasts** contain the green pigment called **chlorophyll**. Chlorophyll absorbs light to enable photosynthesis to take place (photosynthesis is explained more fully in Revision Session 4, pages 59-61). Root cells do not contain chloroplasts as they are not exposed to sunlight.

- **Starch grains** are the most common food store of the plant cell. The plant stores glucose made by photosynthesis in the form of starch.

- Animal cells have a wide variety of different shapes, but plant cells are more often a box-like shape and generally show less variety of cell shape. We can summarise the differences between animal and plant cells in the table below:

Structures present in both plant and animal cells	Structures present only in plant cells
nucleus	cell wall
cytoplasm	chloroplasts
cell membrane	large vacuole

CHECK YOURSELF QUESTIONS

Q1 Draw and label a typical animal cell.

Q2 Make a list of all the parts that animal and plant cells have in common.

Q3 Here is a diagram of a plant cell from a leaf. Complete the diagram by adding the names of each of the labelled parts.

Q4 Copy and complete this table of differences between plant and animal cells.

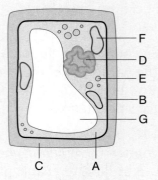

Plant cells have	Animal cells have

What you should already know

- Plants need light for growth.

- The importance of the leaf in absorbing light.

- That plants in food chains are described as producers.

- The main functions of some organs of plants.

- How these functions are essential to the plants.

WHAT YOU NEED TO KNOW

- Animals get their food by eating other animals or plants (or both). Plants do not feed in this way. Plants grow by producing biomass (biological mass). This is done by using light energy to turn water and carbon dioxide into **glucose** (a type of sugar). This process is called **photosynthesis**. Oxygen gas is made as a waste product. This might seem a little strange because we usually think of oxygen as being a very useful gas and not as a waste product. The oxygen produced may be used up in respiration (see Unit 3 Revision Session 4, pages 103-105) or it may pass out of the leaf.

- Photosynthesis is not quite as simple as this. If we shine light onto carbon dioxide and water, will glucose and oxygen be made? Of course not! There are very complicated structures inside green plant cells that make photosynthesis happen in the way that it does. The leaf is a biomass factory, specially designed to make glucose and starch as efficiently as possible.

THE STRUCTURE AND FUNCTION OF THE LEAF

- Photosynthesis takes place in all of the green parts of plants. In most plants, the leaves are the major site of photosynthesis. The leaves are adapted to make them the most effective site for photosynthesis.

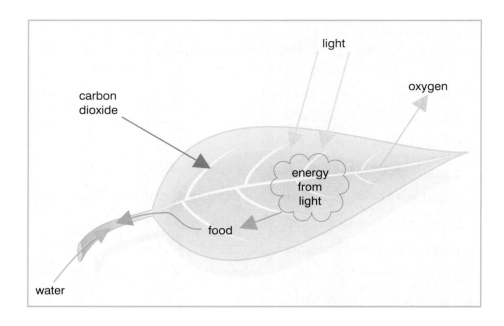

The leaf is a good site for photosynthesis because:
- the leaf contains many specialised cells that are packed with **chloroplasts**. The chloroplasts contain the green substance **chlorophyll**. Chlorophyll absorbs sunlight and makes this energy available for the process of photosynthesis.
- the leaf has a large **surface area**, so it is able to absorb sunlight more efficiently.
- the leaf has many tiny holes in it called **stomata** which allow carbon dioxide to pass in and oxygen to pass out during the day.
- **veins** carry water into the leaf from the roots. The part of the plant's veins that carries water is called the **xylem**.

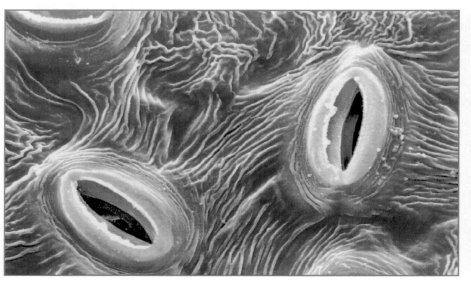

This magnified view of the undersurface of a leaf shows open stomata

Veins carry water through the leaf

- We can write down what happens in photosynthesis in a shorthand way as a word equation (this will be dealt with in more detail in the Revision Session 6, *Word Equations*).

$$\text{carbon dioxide + water} \xrightarrow{\text{light energy}} \text{glucose + oxygen}$$

- In the presence of light, carbon dioxide and water react to produce glucose and oxygen. The rate at which glucose is produced depends on the amounts of carbon dioxide, water and light present.

- The plant can use the glucose it makes during photosynthesis in several ways:
  - glucose is used in respiration (see pages 103–105, *Respiration*);
  - glucose can be changed into starch, which is stored for use later;
  - glucose can be built up into other large molecules such as cellulose or protein. These substances are used for growth and repair of the plant.

? CHECK YOURSELF QUESTIONS

Q1 How do plants produce biomass?

Q2 Photosynthesis is a process. It has inputs (raw materials needed by the process) and outputs (things that the process makes). Complete the following table with the inputs and outputs of photosynthesis.

Inputs	Outputs

Q3 List four reasons why the leaf is a good site for photosynthesis.

Q4 a Write a word equation to summarise photosynthesis.

b A market gardener grows tomatoes in a greenhouse. Suggest ways that she can make the tomato plants grow faster so that she can get large, ripe tomatoes to market earlier than the other local tomato growers.

What you should already know

- Different organs of the body work together in systems.

- The body needs a range of different foodstuffs to keep it working well.

WHAT YOU NEED TO KNOW

A BALANCED DIET

- As well as **proteins**, **carbohydrates** and **fat**, the body needs a range of vitamins and minerals in order to stay healthy.

  - **Calcium** is needed for healthy bones and teeth – we get that from milk and cheese.
  - **Iron** is needed for making red blood cells – we get this from red meat.
  - The **fibre** we get from fruit, vegetables and cereals is needed to keep the food moving smoothly along the digestive system.

- Vitamins are also essential in our diet.

Vitamin A	Helps you see in the dark.
Vitamin B	Is important in the chemical reactions of respiration.
Vitamin C	Is needed for healthy skin and gums.
Vitamin D	Is needed to help the body make use of calcium to grow healthy bones and teeth.

- The food we eat is broken down by the organs of our digestive system.

- As well as eating a **balanced diet** we must avoid substances that can harm our bodies such as alcohol, cigarettes and drugs.

- Alcohol can damage the liver if this organ has to break down too much of it – it can also increase your chances of heart disease, stomach ulcers and brain damage. Drinking alcohol will make your reactions slower so it is important not to operate machinery or drive a car when you have been drinking alcohol. This is why it is illegal to drink and drive!

- Cigarettes contain a number of harmful substances which can damage the lungs and block the arteries. Smokers have a much higher risk of developing cancers of the mouth, throat and lungs as well as heart disease and breathing disorders.

- If a pregnant woman drinks or smokes or takes drugs then these substances will cross the placenta, along with food and oxygen, and pass into the bloodstream of her unborn baby.

DISEASE

- As well as being harmed by substances that are not good for our bodies, we are also at risk from micro-organisms that can cause diseases. There are four main types of **micro-organisms**.

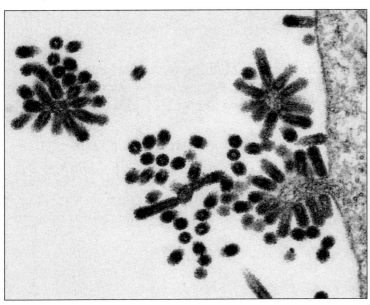

virus

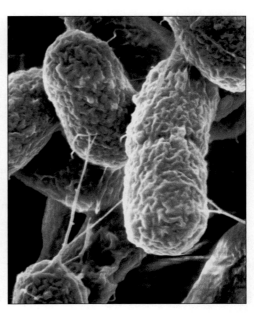

bacteria

- **Viruses** are the smallest. They survive by living inside the cells of other living organisms and destroying these cells. Viruses are responsible for diseases such as 'flu, measles and chicken pox.

- **Bacteria** are single-celled organisms that live between the cells in body tissues. They are responsible for serious illnesses like tuberculosis (TB), pneumonia and cholera, as well as more common illnesses like tonsillitis. The salmonella bacteria can be a cause of food poisoning if they grow in foodstuffs which are then eaten. Bacteria need food and warmth to grow and are killed by very high temperatures. Food is stored in cold conditions such as in a refrigerator or freezer in order to slow the growth of bacteria. Raw food, and re-heated cooked food, should be cooked at high temperatures to kill bacteria.

protozoa

fungi

- **Protozoa** are much larger micro-organisms which cause diseases such as malaria and amoebic dysentery.

- **Fungi** are the largest of all the micro-organisms. The mould we see on rotting food is a fungus, and fungi cause athlete's foot and ringworm. The antibiotic drug penicillin which you might be given by the doctor to cure a bacterial disease is also a fungus.

IMMUNISATION

- Our bodies have a means of protecting us from diseases. It is called the **immune system**. This system produces chemicals called **antibodies** which attack bacteria and viruses in our bodies and enable us to get well again.

- When we have an injection to protect us from a disease such as measles or tuberculosis, this is a way of stimulating our bodies to produce the antibodies needed to fight these diseases. This means that when we come into contact with the bacteria, or virus, our bodies are ready to deal with the disease and we do not become ill. This is called **immunisation**.

? CHECK YOURSELF QUESTIONS

Q1 Why does a fifteen-year-old boy need more protein in his diet that a man of 35?

Q2 Why does a girl of 16 need more iron in her diet than a boy of the same age?

Q3 Sarah had tonsillitis so she went to the doctor and was given some antibiotics. That evening she rang her friend to find out what she had missed at school that day. Her friend was surprised because three weeks ago when she went to see the doctor with 'flu symptoms, she had been told to go home keep warm and drink plenty of fluids. Sarah was able to explain to her friend why she had been given antibiotics when her friend had not. What did Sarah say?

Q4 What is the name of the organ by which a mother passes food and oxygen to her unborn baby?

- Chemical substances have names and these can often tell you which chemical elements they contain.

- In any chemical reaction new and different substances are produced from the reacting substances.

- Useful products can be made from chemical reactions.

WHAT YOU NEED TO KNOW

- All matter is made of tiny particles called **atoms**. There are about 100 different types of atom. A substance that is made of just one type of atom is called an **element**.

- You have probably heard the names of the most common elements, such as oxygen, hydrogen, iron and carbon. Most of the substances around us contain more than one type of atom.

- Atoms of different elements can join together in a chemical reaction to form a **compound**. Water is a compound of hydrogen atoms and oxygen atoms. Elements are like building blocks which join together in different combinations to form different compounds.

- We can use a word equation to give a simple summary of a chemical reaction between two or more substances. It contains only the names of the substances which are involved in the reaction.

- To write accurate word equations you will have to be familiar with the names of chemical substances. The names of some important elements are written below.

Metals	Symbol	Non-metals	Symbol
sodium	Na	hydrogen	H
potassium	K	nitrogen	N
magnesium	Mg	oxygen	O
calcium	Ca	sulphur	S
aluminium	Al	chlorine	Cl
iron	Fe	neon	Ne
copper	Cu	argon	Ar
zinc	Zn		
silver	Ag		
gold	Au		

The symbol for each element is the shorter version of its name. Symbols are used in chemical equations.

UNDERSTANDING CHEMICAL NAMES

- Compounds contain either a metal with non-metals, or just non-metals. You can get a good idea of what elements are contained in a compound from the way the name is written:

  magnesium oxide contains **magnesium** and **oxygen**
  magnesium chloride contains **magnesium** and **chlorine**

- The names seem to be logical apart from what has happened to the ending of the word. The ending gives some more information.

- The ending '**-ide**' tells you that there are only two elements in the compound. The first example above contains only magnesium and oxygen. In the second example, only magnesium and chlorine are present.

- Some compounds end in '**-ate**', such as copper sulphate. This ending indicates that there are three elements present and one of them will be oxygen.

  For example:

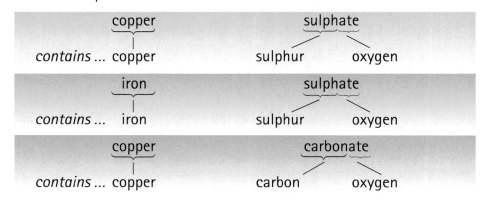

Here are a few more examples.

Compound	Elements
iron ox<u>ide</u>	iron and oxygen
iron sulph<u>ide</u>	iron and sulphur
iron sulph<u>ate</u>	iron and sulphur and oxygen
sodium chlor<u>ide</u>	sodium and chlorine
sodium nitr<u>ate</u>	sodium and nitrogen and oxygen

- The names of some other substances give different information about the chemical composition of the substance:

  carbon dioxide is made up of two ('di' = two) lots of oxygen for every one lot of carbon;

  carbon monoxide contains only one ('mono' = one) lot of oxygen for one lot of carbon.

- However, there are some substances with common names that do not give any clues about which elements they contain. For example, the name water gives no clue that it is made up of two lots of hydrogen for every one lot of oxygen. Sugar and marble are other examples of this type of name although they both have chemical names.

WORD EQUATIONS

- When you write a word equation, only the names of the substances involved in the reaction and the names of the substances produced are important. Word equations must be written in a very specific and particular way. On the left-hand side, you write the names of the starting substances which take part in the reaction. These are called the **reactants**. On the right-hand side you write the names of all the substance produced as a result of the reaction. These are called the **products**. For example:

methane + oxygen → carbon dioxide + water

- When methane (natural gas) burns in oxygen (contained in air) the reaction produces carbon dioxide and water. Methane and oxygen are the reactants; carbon dioxide and water are the products. The arrow points from the reactants to the products with the + sign meaning 'and'. So this word equation reads like this:

methane *and* oxygen *react to produce* carbon dioxide *and* water

- A word equation only provides a summary of the names of the substances that take part in the reaction and its products. A word equation does not provide any information about:
  - the physical states of the reactants and products (whether they are solid, liquid, gas or a solution);
  - the quantities of the substances reacting and of the products;
  - the energy changes that take place during the reaction;
  - the rate of the reaction;
  - any special conditions necessary for the reaction to take place.

? **CHECK YOURSELF QUESTIONS**

Q1 When calcium metal is put into water, calcium hydroxide and hydrogen gas are produced. Complete this word equation:

calcium + ... → calcium hydroxide + ...

Q2 When magnesium burns in oxygen, magnesium oxide is produced. Complete this word equation:

.... + oxygen → ....

Q3 When magnesium reacts with hydrochloric acid, magnesium chloride and hydrogen are produced. Write a word equation to summarise this reaction.

Q4 During photosynthesis in plants, carbon dioxide and water react to produce glucose and oxygen. Write a word equation for this reaction.

Particles

WHAT YOU NEED TO KNOW

- In order to explain our ideas we often use scientific models. A scientific model helps us to understand a new idea by comparing it with something we already know about. We can then use the scientific model to predict the behaviour of things we haven't seen before. One useful model is the **particle model**.

- Scientists think of materials as being made up of very tiny particles, too small to be seen. If we could split up any substance into smaller and smaller pieces, we would eventually find the particles that make it.

- You might think of particles this way. Imagine you are standing on a beach. If you look closely, you would be able to see the individual grains of sand. If you looked around, you would see the whole beach made of sand. Now imagine you are taking off in a helicopter above the beach – first you would see the sand swirling about, but as you get higher, you would not be able to see the individual grains of sand. All you would see is that it is yellow and it is a sandy beach.

- It is like that with particles – you cannot see each one, but when there are enough of them close together they make a substance that you can see. We can use this particle model to represent a solid, a liquid and a gas.

- In a solid, the particles are very close together. We draw them touching which means that they are fixed together. They make up a **regular** pattern. The particles move slightly – they vibrate in their fixed positions, they do not move about from one place to another.

solid

liquid
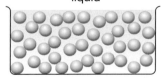

gas
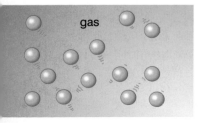

- In a liquid, the particles start to move away from each other. They are not all fixed together – only some of them are still touching. They are not arranged in any particular pattern. The particles are moving randomly about from one place to another.

- In a gas, the particles are a long way apart from each other and move very rapidly in all directions. They show **random** movement and collide with each other as they move.

EXPANSION AND CONTRACTION

- Supplying energy to the particles increases the amount of movement in the particles. The effect is that the particles move further apart, so the whole substance takes up more space – it expands. If energy is removed (by cooling) the particles move closer together and the material contracts.

expanded

contracted

- By supplying more energy, a solid will melt and form a liquid. If even more energy is supplied to the particles, the movement will be even greater and the liquid can become a gas. If you remove energy (by cooling), a gas can become a liquid (e.g. water vapour condensing to form liquid water), and a liquid can become a solid (e.g. liquid water freezing to form ice).

THE ROCK CYCLE

- Expansion, contraction, melting and solidifying are important processes in the rock cycle. There are three groups of rock – **igneous**, **sedimentary** and **metamorphic**.

  - **Igneous rocks** are formed when magma (molten rock from inside the Earth) cools. They are very hard and have a speckled appearance. An example of an igneous rock is granite.

  - **Sedimentary rocks** are formed when sediments, such as sand and mud, settle out and are compressed and cemented together under the weight of the sediment above. Sedimentary rocks are layered and often contain fossils. An example of a sedimentary rock is sandstone.

  - **Metamorphic rocks** are formed when existing rocks are changed by the considerable heat and pressure under the earth. They have a streaky or layered appearance. An example of a metamorphic rock is slate.

CHECK YOURSELF QUESTIONS

Q1 Draw a diagram and describe the arrangement of particles in:

  a a solid;

  b a liquid;

  c a gas.

Q2 Describe the movement of particles and the arrangement of particles in the following changes:

  a melting;

  b the expansion of a solid;

  c condensation.

Q3 Describe how metamorphic rocks are formed.

> **What you should already know**
>
> • Changes of state are reversible changes.
>
> • Chemical reactions can be written in the form of word equations.

WHAT YOU NEED TO KNOW

• Changes that take place in chemical reactions are called **chemical changes**. Changes such as evaporation and condensation that do not involve a chemical reaction are called **physical changes**. The differences between chemical changes and physical changes are summarised in the table below:

Physical changes	Chemical changes
do not form a new substance	form a new substance
do not release large amounts of energy	sometimes release large amounts of energy
can be changed back quite easily	cannot be changed back easily

• If you study some chemical reactions, you can spot **patterns** in the way that some groups of substances react with other groups. A good example is the reaction between acids and indicators.

• If you put **Universal Indicator** into an acidic solution, the indicator will turn red. It does not matter which acid you use – all acids turn Universal Indicator red. Alkalis turn Universal Indicator shades of blue to purple and neutral solutions will turn the indicator green.

• We measure acids and alkalis on a scale called the **pH scale**. Strong **acids** have a pH of 1 or 2, weaker acids have a pH of 3 to 5 or 6 and **neutral solutions** have a pH of 7. High pH values show that a solution is **alkaline** – the strongest alkalis having a pH of around 14.

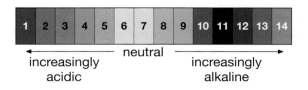

| 1 | 2 | 3 | 4 | 5 | 6 | 7 | 8 | 9 | 10 | 11 | 12 | 13 | 14 |

increasingly acidic ← → neutral ← → increasingly alkaline

- Many foodstuffs are quite strong acids such as lemon juice, vinegar and many fizzy drinks. Detergents and cleaning products are generally alkaline. Soaps and hair shampoos are mild alkalis and strong household cleaners, especially bleach, are strong alkalis. Water is neutral so pure water will have a pH of 7.

ACID AND ALKALI REACTIONS

acid   neutral   alkali

- When an acid reacts with an alkali, the resulting solution will have a pH somewhere between the pH values of the two reactants. This means that an alkaline solution can be used to reduce the acidity of a solution or to **neutralise** an acid completely. An example of this is when too much stomach acid causes someone to suffer from a burning sensation known as indigestion. Remedies for this are all alkaline and, if swallowed in the correct amount, can reduce the excess acidity and relieve the pain without neutralising completely the stomach acid that is essential for digestion.

- Farmers and gardeners will sometimes add either acidic or alkaline chemicals to soil to create the correct pH for a particular plant to grow. Some plants like an acidic soil, some like neutral soil and some prefer alkaline conditions. Careful testing of the pH of the soil and adding the right chemicals can create the perfect environment!

Rhododendron (acidic soil)   *Cherry tree (alkaline soil)*

ACIDS AND METALS

- The reactions between metals and acids are all very similar and can be summarised in this word equation:

metal + acid → metal salt + hydrogen

For example:
calcium + hydrochloric acid → calcium chloride + hydrogen

magnesium + sulphuric acid → magnesium sulphate + hydrogen

- Hydrogen is produced in all of these reactions but the time it takes for the reaction to happen is different for each type of metal and each type of acid. Some metals react very quickly, some are slower and some react so slowly they can hardly be seen to react

Magnesium, calcium and lead in dilute acid

at all. This is an example of a **trend** in properties. The reactions are very similar – they all produce hydrogen – but there is a difference in speed of reaction from one metal to another.

ACIDS AND CARBONATES

- There is also a pattern in the way acids react with compounds called carbonates. Each of these reactions produces carbon dioxide. The reaction between acids and carbonates can be summarised by the word equation:

acid + metal carbonate → metal salt + carbon dioxide + water

Some examples of such reaction are:

hydrochloric acid + calcium carbonate → calcium chloride + carbon dioxide + water

sulphuric acid + sodium carbonate → sodium sulphate + carbon dioxide + water

CHECK YOURSELF QUESTIONS

Q1 What is the pH of these substances likely to be:

a water;

b fizzy cola drink;

c orange juice;

d toilet cleaner?

Q2 Which of the following are physical changes and which are chemical changes:

a melting ice;

b burning a fuel;

c magnesium and acid reacting together;

d condensation forming on a window?

Q3 What gas is produced when an acid reacts with a metal carbonate?

Oxidation Reactions

What you should already know

- The difference between chemical reactions and physical changes.

- Chemical reactions such as burning and rusting are non-reversible changes.

WHAT YOU NEED TO KNOW

- Chemical reactions that take in oxygen are known as **oxidation reactions.**

METALS AND OXYGEN

- Nearly all metals react with the oxygen in air. When they do this they lose their shine and go dull (they 'tarnish'). Some metals like sodium will do this in a few seconds. Others take much longer.

Aluminium (top) and magnesium scratched to show a shiny surface

- The time it takes for different metals to tarnish is another trend. When a metal reacts with oxygen it forms a chemical compound called an **oxide**. Iron forms iron oxide which is more commonly known as rust. Magnesium and aluminium also react with oxygen in the air to form an oxide, resulting in a dull looking layer on the surface of the metal.

- Millions of years ago, the metallic elements that were formed in the Earth reacted with oxygen in the atmosphere to form oxides. These oxides are still present and they are the source of metals that are used in industry. The metal compounds in the earth are called **ores**.

- A metal can be extracted from its ore by carrying out a chemical reaction. Oxygen is removed in the reaction, leaving the pure metal.

COMBUSTION AND RESPIRATION

- **Combustion** describes the reaction that happens when any substance burns in oxygen.

  - When fuels burn in air to release heat energy this is an oxidation reaction. You can put out a fire by smothering it because burning needs oxygen.

  - Fossil fuels, coal, oil and natural gas, are so called because they were made from the remains of prehistoric animals and plants – chemically they are made up mostly of carbon and hydrogen. These two elements burn well and compounds made from them are capable of producing a lot of heat energy when they are burnt.

Burning fossil fuels — coal, methane (natural gas) and oil

- Like all chemical reactions the products at the end can be very different from the reactants that went into the reaction in the beginning.

- **Respiration** is an example of an oxidation reaction of a non-metallic compound. Think of the word equation for respiration:

  glucose + oxygen $\rightarrow$ carbon dioxide + water PLUS ENERGY

- This is another example of an oxidation reaction where energy is given out.

? CHECK YOURSELF QUESTIONS

Q1 Write a word equation to describe what happens when magnesium reacts with air.

Q2 Which two elements are most common in fossil fuels and what is the chemical symbol for each of these elements?

Q3 What are the products of respiration?

Forces and Motion

> **What you should already know**
>
> - A force can be a push or a pull.
> - Unbalanced forces make objects change speed or direction or shape.

WHAT YOU NEED TO KNOW

- When the forces on an object are balanced it will either stay still OR, if it is already moving, it will continue to move at a steady speed in the same direction.

- Forces on objects can be shown by arrows which represent both the size and the direction of the force.

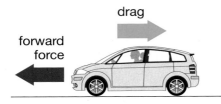

drag

forward force

The forces on this car are the same. It will continue to move at a steady speed in a constant direction.

On this car the force pushing it forward is much greater than the force slowing it down so its speed will be increasing.

drag

forward force

CALCULATING SPEED

- We can calculate the speed of a moving object using this equation:

$$speed = \frac{distance}{time}$$

For a journey it is usual to calculate the average speed (which is the total distance travelled divided by the total time taken) rather than working out the speed for each individual part of the journey. It is possible to describe a journey using a distance–time graph which shows how fast you were travelling at various points on the journey. It might look like this.

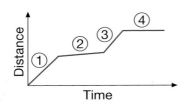

Distance / Time

① – Steady speed
② – Speed became slower
③ – Speed increased
④ – Stationary

CHECK YOURSELF QUESTIONS

Q1 Look at the diagrams below and match each description of the motion to the correct diagram.

car accelerating

car slowing down

car moving at steady speed

Q2 Calculate the missing numbers by using the equation: speed = distance/time. Complete the table.

Speed in metres per second (m/s)	Distance in metres (m)	Time in seconds (s)
	100	50
	500	20
15	150	
30		300

N.B. You might find it easier work out how to calculate distance and time if you use this triangle.

Cover up the quantity you are trying to calculate and it will show you whether to multiply or divide.

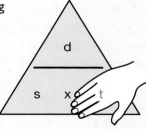

distance = speed x time

time = distance / speed

speed = distance / time

WHAT YOU NEED TO KNOW

- When light passes from one transparent medium (material) to another it almost always changes direction. If you look at a frosted glass window, the objects on the other side of the glass always look distorted. What you see through the glass is different from the real object because the frosted glass affects the light passing through it.

- Frosted glass has a pattern created by changes in the surface and thickness of the glass sheet. Because of the variation in the surface of the glass, individual rays of light have their direction changed by different amounts. This causes the effect that you can see in the photograph on the left.

- The process which causes light to change direction when it passes from one transparent medium to another is called **refraction**. For example, when light travelling in air enters a block of glass it changes direction. Refraction also takes place when light passes from water into air.

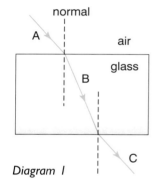

Diagram 1

- Diagram 1 shows a ray of light travelling from air into glass and out into air again. When a ray of light, **A**, passes from air into glass, the ray changes direction getting closer to the **normal**. The normal is a line drawn at right angles (90°) to the surface of the glass at the point the light ray enters or leaves the glass block. When the ray leaves the block it changes direction again getting further away from the normal. The rays of light at **A** and **C** are **parallel** to each other.

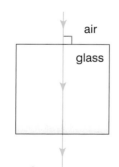

Diagram 2

- The ray of light in diagram 2 is not refracted because it enters the glass block at right angles to its surface (in other words, along the normal). This is the only situation in which refraction does not occur when light enters another transparent medium.

- When a ray of light passes from air into Perspex, it travels from a less-dense medium into a more-dense medium. Light slows down as it enters the more dense Perspex. Look at Diagram 3 and think about the ray entering the Perspex. Because it is entering the Perspex at an angle of less than 90°, point **A** of this ray reaches the Perspex and is slowed down before point **B.** This means that in the time it takes for the top part of the ray to move from **B** to **D**, the bottom part of the ray only moves from **A** to **C**. The ray has travelled a shorter distance inside the block than outside. We say it has been **refracted**.

Diagram 3

ANOTHER WAY OF LOOKING AT REFRACTION

- A model of this situation, which may help you to understand refraction, is a car driving off a smooth road into a muddy patch.

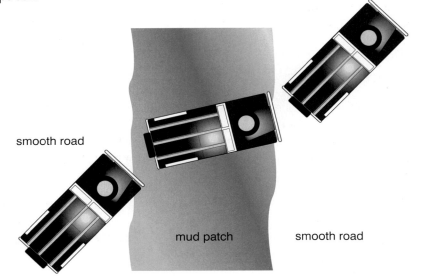

smooth road

mud patch   smooth road

- When the car reaches the muddy patch, the front right-hand tyre reaches the mud first, so it slows down before the left-hand tyre reaches the mud. This pulls the car to the right. It will then travel through the mud in a straight line. When the car leaves the patch of mud, the right-hand tyre reaches the smooth road first, so it will then move quicker than the left-hand tyre. The car pulls out of the patch of mud and moves away to the left. If you think of the ray of light moving in a similar way to the car, it may help you to understand refraction.

- When light travels from a less-dense medium to a more-dense medium (e.g. from air to glass), the light is refracted *towards* the normal. When light travels from a more-dense medium to less-dense medium (e.g. from glass to air), it is refracted *away from* the normal.

- The amount of refraction that occurs when a ray of light passes from one medium to another depends on the material through which the light is passing. Each transparent material has a different density so it will refract rays of light by different amounts.

- Sometimes the rays of light are drawn showing **wavefronts**, which look like a pattern of straight waves produced in a ripple tank. In this diagram, you can see how to represent what happens to rays of light that are drawn this way.

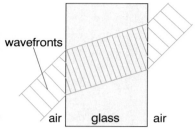

- As the wavefronts enter the glass they are slowed down. The remaining part of the wavefront, still moving through the air, continues at the same speed. This part of the wavefront travels further in the same time and so the ray of light is refracted towards the normal line.

? CHECK YOURSELF QUESTIONS

Q1 a Complete this diagram to show how a ray of light passes through a Perspex block.

air

perspex

b Draw another ray of light on your diagram which will pass through the block without being refracted.

c What name is given to the process which causes rays of light to change direction?

Q2 Anna has come to feed her goldfish in the garden pond. Find out whether or not she can see the goldfish by drawing a ray of light from the goldfish to Anna. Can she see the goldfish?

What you should already know

- There are a variety of energy resources, including coal, oil, gas, biomass, wind, waves and batteries.

- Some of the Earth's energy resources are renewable and some are not.

WHAT YOU NEED TO KNOW

- We use huge amounts of energy to run our homes, schools, factories and for transport. Much of the energy comes from coal, oil and gas. These are called **fossil fuels**. Fossil fuels were formed from dead plants and animals that lived many millions of years ago.

- There is only a limited supply of fossil fuels in the Earth's crust. If we continue to use them at the present rate, some scientists have predicted that there is only enough coal to last about 300 years and enough oil and gas to last about 50 years.

- All of the energy contained within these energy resources came originally from the Sun. All of the plants that were turned into coal used energy from the Sun – in the form of light – to produce glucose and oxygen from carbon dioxide and water (see Unit 2 Revision Session 4 pages 59–61, *Photosynthesis*). All of the animals that were turned into oil and gas got their food from plants. This means that the Sun is the source of most of the Earth's energy resources.

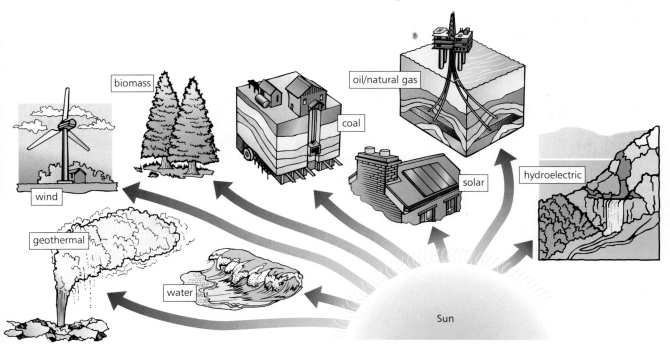

- Today energy that can be used for domestic or industrial purposes comes from a wide range of sources. Some of these are shown in the diagram on page 81.

- Plants need energy from the Sun to grow. Animals take advantage of this energy directly by eating plants or indirectly by eating animals that have eaten plants. When fossil fuels are burnt, the energy (that originally came from the Sun) is released.

- Many power stations generate electricity by burning fossil fuels. The flow chart on the left shows – in a simplified way – what happens inside a thermal power station.

- The Earth's supply of fossil fuels is limited. We can extend the time that they will last by developing other ways of producing electricity.

ALTERNATIVE ENERGY RESOURCES

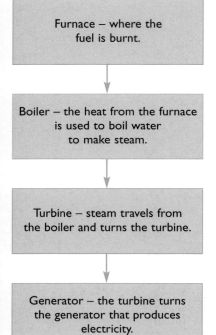

Furnace – where the fuel is burnt.

Boiler – the heat from the furnace is used to boil water to make steam.

Turbine – steam travels from the boiler and turns the turbine.

Generator – the turbine turns the generator that produces electricity.

- **Biomass** is any plant or animal material that can be used as a fuel or to produce a fuel. Wood, methane (from decaying animal and plant material) and alcohol (made from sugar) are all biomass. They can all be burnt in the furnace of a power station. Alcohol can also be used to provide fuel for cars.

- **Wind** is caused by the Sun heating air in some areas more than others. The hot air rises and cool air takes its place. The movement of air in the atmosphere is called wind. Wind can be captured by the blades of large windmills. In exposed areas, hundreds of these windmills (called 'aerogenerators') make up a wind farm. The wind provides energy to drive the windmill that turns a generator to produce electricity.

- **Waves** are caused by wind blowing across the sea. The rocking motion of waves can be used to drive generators. One type is the 'nodding duck'. It consists of a line of floats that are fixed on one side, allowing the other side to nod up and down with the waves. A pump is driven by the nodding action, pushing water through a turbine to drive a generator.

- **Hydroelectric power** uses the flow of water down a hill to drive turbines. Rain water that has fallen high in mountains can be trapped in a reservoir and then allowed to flow downhill through pipes. Turbines at the bottom of the pipes are driven by the flow of water and they turn generators to produce electricity.

- **Solar energy** can be collected by using solar cells, solar panels and solar furnaces. Solar cells produce electricity from chemicals when light falls onto them. Solar panels use heat from the Sun to produce hot water. Solar furnaces use many mirrors to direct heat from the Sun onto a water tank. The water boils, producing steam, which can be used to drive turbines.

- The alternative energy resources we have dealt with so far come directly or indirectly from the Sun and are renewable. There are, however, some energy resources that do not come from the Sun.

- **Nuclear energy** is used to heat water to produce steam, which drives a turbine. Radioactive materials, such as uranium, undergo nuclear reaction. As a result of this, they give out a lot of energy. Nuclear energy is non-renewable – the radioactive materials in the Earth's crust that are used in nuclear reactors will eventually run out.

- **Geothermal energy** is energy from hot rocks deep inside the Earth's crust. Water can be pumped down to the hot rocks where it turns to steam. The steam is used to generate electricity.

- **Tidal energy** uses the tides to generate electricity. Tides are caused by the pull of the Moon on the Earth. At high tide, water flows behind a barrage where it is trapped. As the water flows back to the sea, it can be used to turn turbines and generate electricity.

CHECK YOURSELF QUESTIONS

Q1 Tick in the correct column of the table to show whether the energy resource is renewable or non-renewable. Put a tick in the last column if the energy has originally come from the Sun.

Energy resource	Renewable	Non-renewable	From the Sun
coal			
oil			
gas			
wave			
tidal			
hydroelectric			
biomass			
nuclear			
solar			
wind			

Q2 Why can't we depend only on wind energy or solar energy in the UK?

Q3 Explain how electricity is made using:

   a a fossil fuel;

   b wind.

The Solar System

> **What you should already know**
>
> - The apparent movement of the Sun and other stars is caused by the movement of the Earth.
> - Luminous objects give out light.
> - We are able to see non-luminous objects because light from a source is reflected from them.

WHAT YOU NEED TO KNOW

- A star is a massive 'ball of fire' which may have planets in orbit around it. A planet is a large object which orbits a star. Any object that orbits a planet is called a moon. Some planets have many moons orbiting them, e.g. Jupiter. The Earth has one moon called the Moon! The star at the centre of our solar system is called the Sun. There are nine planets in orbit around the Sun.

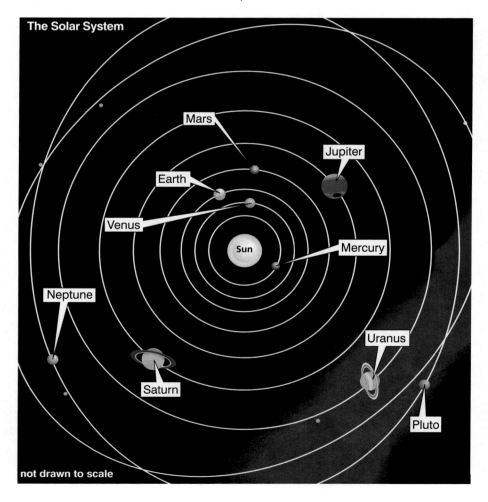

The Solar System

Mars
Jupiter
Earth
Venus
Sun
Mercury
Neptune
Uranus
Saturn
Pluto

not drawn to scale

- Starting with the planet nearest the Sun, the order of the planets is: Mercury, Venus, Earth, Mars, Jupiter, Saturn, Uranus, Neptune and Pluto. To help you remember the order of the planets you can make up a funny sentence of words starting with the first letters of the planets (for example, you could try: Most Vegetarians Eat Many Jam Sandwiches Under Nine Planets).

STARS AND PLANETS

- Stars such as our Sun give out heat and light. There are many other stars much further away from the Earth that also give out heat and light. On a clear night you can see thousands of stars in the sky.

- The planets do not give out light; they are illuminated by the star that they orbit. Earth is lit by the Sun. We can sometimes see some other planets in our solar system shining brightly in the sky. This is because they reflect the light from the Sun. The further away the planet is from Earth, the less bright it will appear. The closer the planet is to the Earth, the brighter it will appear.

- Astronomers have found that different coloured light is produced by different stars. The colour of a star indicates its temperature. Some stars are very hot (20 000°C at the surface) and shine with a blue light. Others are much cooler and look red.

- The brightest star in the sky, Sirius, looks white and is very hot (approximately 10 000°C). The Sun is yellow. It is a medium hot star at approximately 6000°C. Proxima Centauri, the nearest known star to the Sun, is a dim red. Its temperature is about 3000°C. The temperature of the star and its distance from the Earth are factors which affect its relative brightness.

Mars taken from a satellite

Stars in the night sky

CHECK YOURSELF QUESTIONS

Q1 Write down a definition of:

a a star;

b a planet;

c a moon.

Q2 a Complete the diagram to show the path taken by Venus as it orbits the Sun.

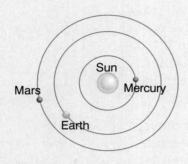

b Draw Venus on the diagram at its furthest point from Earth.

When the planets are in the positions shown:

c can Mercury be seen from Earth?

d can Mars be seen from Earth?

Give a reason for your answers in c and d.

Q3 Put the following in order of temperature starting with the hottest:

Earth   Sun   a white star
a blue star   a red star

1 **a** The drawings show a stoat in summer and in winter.

In winter the ground is often covered by snow or frost. During this part of the year a stoat's fur is white.

stoat in summer   stoat in winter

Suggest **two** ways its white coat helps a stoat to survive in the winter.

....

....   *(2 marks)*

b The diagram shows the family tree for a family of rabbits.

Use words from the list below to complete the sentences.

**adapt   cytoplasm
genes   grow   inherit
letters   membrane
mutate   nuclei**

Rabbits have the same fur colour all year round.

Young rabbits ....fur colour from their parents. Information

about fur colour is passed on from one generation to the next in the form

of .... in the ....of an egg and sperm.   *(3 marks)*

maximum 5 marks

2 The diagram below shows a cell from the inside of a human cheek.

a On the diagram, label parts A, B and C.

(3 marks)

b Plant cells have some parts which animal cells do **not** have. Name **two** of these parts.

A ....

B ....

C ....

1 ....

2 ....

(2 marks)

c The diagram on the right shows a cell from a leaf of a blackberry plant.

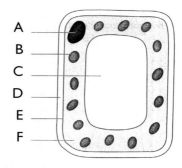

The names of four parts of the cell are listed in the table below.

(i) Match the name of each part with a letter from the diagram.

Write your answers in the table.

(4 marks)

part	letter of part
cell wall	
cytoplasm	
nucleus	
vacuole	

(ii) Which **two** of the labelled parts are also present in an animal cell?

Give the correct letters from the diagram.

.... and .... *(2 marks)*

maximum 11 marks

3 The drawing shows part of a blackberry plant.

a Photosynthesis takes place in the leaves of the blackberry plant.

Complete the word equation for photosynthesis.

Water + carbon dioxide → .... + oxygen

(1 mark)

b Jonathan studied a blackberry plant growing in a shady place and a blackberry plant growing in a sunny place.

(i) Jonathan found that the plant in the shady place had larger leaves. Why is it an advantage for plants in the shade to have leaves with a large surface area?

....

.... *(1 mark)*

(ii) Both blackberry plants had green leaves. What part of the leaf cells makes the leaf green?

.... *(1 mark)*

maximum 3 marks

4 An experiment was set up to investigate rusting. Some clean, shiny, iron nails were sealed in a glass bottle containing some tap water. The sealed bottle was then placed on a top-pan balance. The reading on the balance was 549.8 g.
The sealed bottle was left for one week.
After one week the nails were rusty.

sealed bottle
tap water
nails

a (i) What would you expect the reading on the balance to be after one week?

.... *(1 mark)*

(ii) Give a reason for your answer.

.... *(1 mark)*

b (i) Rust is an oxide of iron. Another oxide of iron is iron (III) oxide. Write a word equation for the formation of iron (III) oxide from its elements.

.... *(1 mark)*

(ii) Which one of the following words describes the formation of iron (III) oxide from its elements?
combustion   condensation   decomposition   oxidation

.... *(1 mark)*

maximum 4 marks

5 Some roads are made of concrete. The concrete is laid in sections with small gaps between them.

concrete section
gap
concrete section
not to scale

a (i) What happens to the size of most objects when they get hotter?

.... *(1 mark)*

(ii) When the temperature rises, what will happen to the gaps between the concrete sections?

.... *(1 mark)*

(iii) When the temperature rises, what might happen to the sections of concrete if there are **no** gaps between them?

.... *(1 mark)*

b The gaps between the concrete sections are filled with tar. The tar becomes soft when it is warm. Why is it important that the tar becomes soft?

.... *(1 mark)*

maximum 4 marks

6 Sailors used to suffer from an illness called scurvy caused by a poor diet on long journeys.

James Lind was a doctor who tested treatments for scurvy. He predicted that **all acids cure scurvy.**

He gave 6 pairs of sailors with scurvy exactly the same meals but he also gave each pair a different addition to their diet.

pair of sailors	addition to their diet	effect after one week
1	some apple cider	beginning to recover
2	25 drops of very dilute sulphuric acid to gargle with*	still had scurvy
3	2 teaspoons of vinegar	still had scurvy
4	half a pint of sea water*	still had scurvy
5	2 oranges and 1 lemon	recovered
6	herbs and spices and acidified barley water	still had scurvy

a Does the evidence in the table support the prediction that all acids cure scurvy? Tick the correct box.

yes ☐   no ☐   * DANGER!
                                         DO NOT TRY THIS

Use the table to explain your answer.

.... *(1 mark)*

b (i) Give the **one** factor James Lind **changed** in this experiment.
(This is called the independent variable.)

.... *(1 mark)*

(ii) Give the factor James Lind **examined** in this experiment.
(This is called the dependent variable.)

.... *(1 mark)*

c James Lind's evidence suggested that oranges and lemons cured scurvy. At a later time, other scientists did the following:
• They separated citric acid from the fruit.
• They predicted that citric acid would cure scurvy.
• They tested their prediction by giving pure citric acid as an addition to the diet of sailors with scurvy.
• They found it did **not** cure scurvy.

The scientists had to make a different prediction.

Suggest a new prediction about a cure for scurvy that is consistent with the evidence collected.

.... *(1 mark)*

d Explain why it is necessary to investigate the effects of changes in diet over a period of more than one week.

.... *(1 mark)*

maximum 5 marks

7 The diagram shows the shapes and positions of five glass objects.

Harriet put a square of black card on top of each glass object. She shone a ray of red light onto each object.

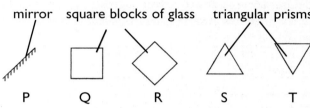

mirror   square blocks of glass   triangular prisms

P   Q   R   S   T

The diagrams show the rays of light going under the cards and coming out again. Which object is under each card? Write the correct letter below each diagram. One has been done for you.

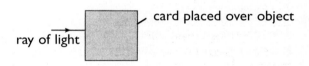

ray of light   card placed over object

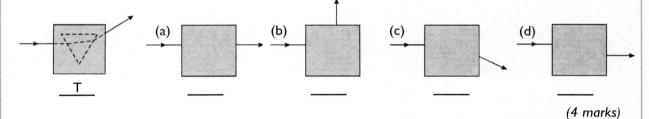

(a)   (b)   (c)   (d)

T   _____   _____   _____   _____

(4 marks)

maximum 4 marks

8 The drawing below shows an astronaut in space. He has four small jets attached to his spacesuit. These jets produce forces on the **astronaut** in the directions A, B, C, and D.

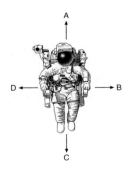

a) The drawing (right) shows the size and direction of four forces acting on the astronaut.

In which direction A, B, C, or D, will the astronaut move?

Give the letter.

....

(1 mark)

10 N

10 N ←   → 10 N

9 N

(b) The drawing below shows the size and direction of four different forces acting on the astronaut. What will happen to the astronaut when the jets produce these four forces?

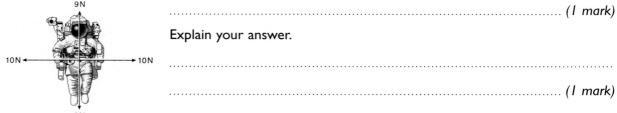

.... *(1 mark)*

Explain your answer.

....

.... *(1 mark)*

(c) The drawing (right) shows the size and direction of four different forces acting on the astronaut.
Draw an arrow on the diagram to show the direction in which he will move.

(1 mark)

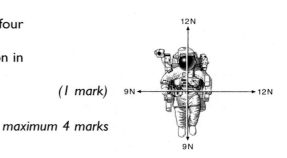

maximum 4 marks

9 The table shows the time taken for the Earth, Mars and Venus to orbit the Sun.

The diagram shows the orbits of the Earth, Mars and Venus round the Sun, at one particular time. The arrows show the direction in which the planets move. At the time shown in the diagram, the three planets were lined up with the Sun.

planet	time taken to orbit the Sun, in Earth years
Earth	1.0
Mars	1.9
Venus	0.6

a Show the position of the Earth **three** months after the planets were lined up, by marking a point on the Earth's orbit. Label the point E. *(1 mark)*

b (i) Show the approximate position of Mars **three** Earth months after the planets were lined up, by marking a point on Mars's orbit. Label the point M. *(1 mark)*

(ii) Explain why Mars is in this position.

.... *(1 mark)*

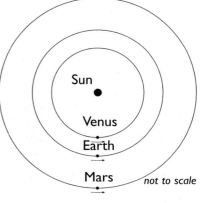

not to scale

c (i) Show the approximate position of Venus **three** Earth months after the planets were lined up, by marking a point on Venus's orbit. Label the point V. *(1 mark)*

(ii) Explain why Venus is in this position.

.... *(1 mark)*

maximum 5 marks

total possible marks 45

total marks [ ]

Scientific Enquiry – Evaluating Evidence

What you should already know

- Scientific ideas and theories always have to be supported by evidence.

WHAT YOU NEED TO KNOW

- Scientific ideas change and develop in the light of new evidence which needs to be both accurate and reliable. Evaluation is the process by which we decide how accurate and reliable a piece of evidence is.

- **Accuracy** is improved by using an appropriate measuring instrument and using it with care.

- **Reliability** is improved by carefully controlling variables apart from the one to be tested. If an experiment is repeated and the results are always the same, then we can say that this is a reliable experiment.

- As well as being accurate and reliable, there has to be enough evidence to support the idea being put forward. Any **conclusion** that is based on many results will always be better than a conclusion based on very few, especially if those results can be shown to be both accurate and reliable.

- In an experiment carried out in a laboratory, it can be quite easy to identify the variables that need to be controlled and to make sure that they are controlled.

- When the experiment is carried out in a real-life situation, then it starts to become harder to control all the variables which might affect the reliability of the evidence.

- For example, in January 2002 the Royal Society for the Protection of Birds carried out a survey into the populations of different kinds of birds living in Britain. To do this, they asked a large number of people to record the numbers of different kinds of birds in their gardens for 1 hour during the last week in January. For the evidence from this survey to be considered reliable, they had to control as many variables that might affect the number of birds as possible.

- In evaluating this survey, it would be possible to say that the time of year and the length of time for which observations had been carried out had been kept the same. This would increase the reliability of the evidence. The exact weather conditions and the time of day were variables that were not controlled and may have had an effect on the number of birds observed.

- With a large number of people taking part, it would not be possible to say how accurate each individual's observations were. However, a large number of participants meant that there was a large amount of data to support any conclusions drawn and that each person's input was a small part of the total picture. This means that individual inaccuracies would not have had too great an effect on the total result.

- All of these things would need to be thought about when evaluating the evidence from this survey. This would help people decide how accurate and reliable a picture of the bird population in Britain in 2002 had been obtained.

CHECK YOURSELF QUESTION

Think about this real-life example of an experiment and decide how you would evaluate what had been done.

In the past, an island off the coast of Scotland had a big problem with slugs. To get rid of the slugs without using chemicals, it was decided to import hedgehogs from the mainland. There had not been any hedgehogs on this island before.

The hedgehogs did seem to help with the slug problem but the island was also home to a number of rare wading seabirds who make their nests on the ground. It was believed that the hedgehogs were responsible for a drop in the numbers of these birds because they ate the eggs from the nests.

It was decided that the hedgehog population needed to be reduced by either catching them and taking them to the mainland, or by killing some or all of them.

a What do you think would be the best thing to do with the hedgehogs?

b Why do you think that?

c When you had made your choice and carried out your plan, how would you evaluate it? What information would you need to collect to show that you had made the right decision?

What you should already know

- Different habitats support different plants and animals.

- Food chains describe the feeding relationships that exist between organisms in a habitat.

- Different organisms are found in different habitats because of differences in environmental factors.

- Environmental factors affect the distribution and abundance of organisms in each habitat.

WHAT YOU NEED TO KNOW

- You should already know that a **habitat** is a place where a plant or an animal lives. **Food chains** show the feeding relationships in a habitat. A simple food chain is shown in the diagram below:

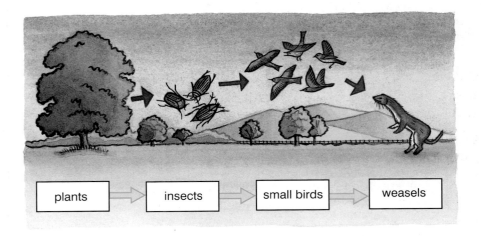

plants		insects		small birds		weasels

- The arrow means 'eaten by' and points towards the organism that does the eating. The arrow shows the direction that food and the energy stored in the food is moving. Food chains do not tell the whole story of what is happening in a habitat because most animals eat a variety of different organisms. A plant or animal usually belongs to several food chains, not just one. So, to get a clear picture of what the feeding relationships are in a habitat, we need to show all of the food chains that there are in that habitat.

- Instead of just making a list of all the food chains, scientists put all the food chain information together to make a food web. An example of a **food web** is shown below.

- Food chains and food webs always start with a plant. The plant at the start of a food chain or food web is called a producer. It is called a **producer** because it makes or produces its own biomass by photosynthesis (see Unit 2, Revision Session 4, *Photosynthesis*). All organisms that come after the producer in the food web are called **consumers**, because they consume (eat) other things to get their food.

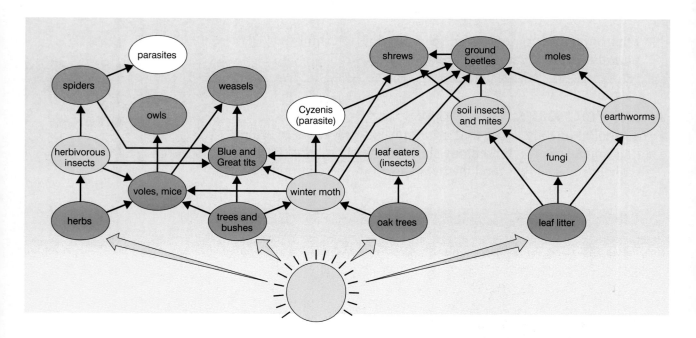

- You will notice that even though voles and mice are involved in several food chains, we only write them down once.

PYRAMIDS OF NUMBERS

- Food webs give us a lot of information about the feeding relationships in any particular habitat. They are much more useful than a simple food chain on its own. But neither food webs nor food chains give us any idea about how many spiders there are in a habitat or how many oak trees there are. When scientists study a habitat, they often count how many organisms there are. They don't usually count every single organism in the habitat because it would take far too long. Instead they take a small area of the habitat (called a 'sample area'). From this sample, they work out how many of each organism there are in the habitat.

- When we know the numbers of organisms in a habitat, we can 'redraw' our food chain as a pyramid. The number of organisms at each level in the pyramid decides the size of each layer of the pyramid:

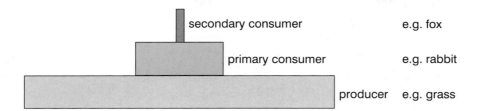

secondary consumer   e.g. fox

primary consumer   e.g. rabbit

producer   e.g. grass

- The size of each level in the pyramid shows the number of organisms at that level. Consumers feeding on plants are called **primary consumers** and the consumers at the next level are called **secondary consumers**. Primary consumers only eat producers (plants) so they are completely 'vegetarian'. Scientists call them **herbivores**. Animals that only eat other animals are called **carnivores**. Animals that eat both plants and other animals are called **omnivores**.

- Usually, as you get higher up the pyramid, there are fewer organisms. There are a number of reasons why this is so. As you get higher up in the pyramid, the organisms often get bigger in size. For example, a fox is bigger than a rabbit, so one fox needs to eat more rabbits than if it was eating bigger organisms. Energy is lost at each stage of the pyramid. A rabbit uses up energy when it moves and keeps its body warm. This means that there is less energy available to the fox.

- A food chain relies on energy from the sun. A plant uses energy from the Sun to produce its biomass. This energy is stored inside the plant, mainly as starch.

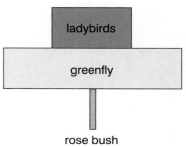

ladybirds

greenfly

rose bush

- Sometimes a pyramid of numbers can be a very different shape. This occurs when the producer is very large in size and mass. Lots of consumers can feed on it because it has lots of energy stored inside it.

CHECK YOURSELF QUESTIONS

Q1 a Draw a food chain with three organisms in it.

b What does a food chain show?

Q2 Study the food web below for a habitat such as a large field in the countryside. Answer the following questions.

a Name one producer.

b Name one consumer.

c Name one herbivore.

d If all the field mice suddenly died, what would happen to the number of dandelions?

e If all the field mice suddenly died, why would the number of foxes be likely to decrease?

f How do you think a reduction in the number of field mice would affect the rabbit population?

g The food chain depends on energy. Where does all the energy come from in the first place?

Q3 Draw a pyramid of numbers for this food chain:

apple tree → moth caterpillars → thrushes
     1   1200   2

Q4 Draw a pyramid of numbers for this food chain:

ladysmock → caterpillars → robin → hawk
  10 000   800   10   1

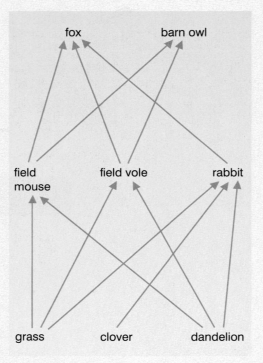

Specialised Cells

> **What you should already know**
>
> • The structure of simple animal and plant cells.
>
> • The differences in structure between simple animal and plant cells.
>
> • The functions of cell membrane, cytoplasm and the nucleus in plant and animal cells.
>
> • The functions of chloroplasts and cell walls in plant cells.

WHAT YOU NEED TO KNOW

• All animal cells have several things in common. They all have a nucleus, a cell membrane and cytoplasm. However, animal cells never have a cell wall or chloroplasts.

• Not all animal cells are the same. Animal cells come in a variety of shapes and sizes.

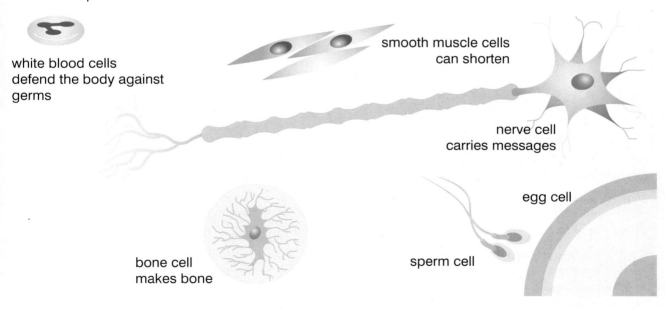

white blood cells defend the body against germs

smooth muscle cells can shorten

nerve cell carries messages

egg cell

sperm cell

bone cell makes bone

• The shape of the cells and their structure depends on their particular function. This is a very important idea in science. Each type of cell is specialised or **adapted** to carry out its function. Cells of the same type gathered together are called tissue, e.g. muscle tissue.

• This session looks at four different types of cell, each of which is specialised to carry out a particular function and shows how their structure allows them to do it.

FACT FILE 1

The sperm cell (animal)

Function

To carry the male genetic information to the ovum (egg cell) and bring about fertilisation. The sperm must swim from the vagina after sexual intercourse, up into the Fallopian tube to join with the ovum (egg cell).

Cell structure and adaptations

The sperm cell is a very highly specialised cell with a number of adaptations that make it very good at carrying out its function:

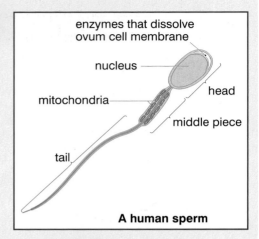

A human sperm

(labels: enzymes that dissolve ovum cell membrane, nucleus, mitochondria, head, middle piece, tail)

Adaptation	How this makes the cell better at its job
tail	allows it to swim from the vagina to the Fallopian tube
nucleus contains only half the genetic information	when it joins the ovum's half genetic information, a full nucleus with a whole set of genetic information will be made
enzymes on the head of the sperm	dissolves quickly through the ovum membrane
lots of mitochondria	provide energy for swimming

FACT FILE 2

Ciliated epithelial cell (animal)

Function

To move liquids or small particles.

Cell structure and adaptations

Cilia are tiny hair-like structures (on the surface of the cell) that the cell can move. We call a cell that has cilia attached to it a ciliated cell. Ciliated epithelial cells are found in the tubes of the respiratory system, e.g. trachea, and bronchi. Ciliated epithelial cells move mucus upwards and away from the lungs.

Adaptation	How this makes the cell better at its job
many cilia	the cilia beat together to move the liquid or particles
many mitochondria in the cell	mitochondria release energy from food and this energy is used to make the cilia move

Root cell hair (plant)

Function

To absorb water and minerals from the soil water.

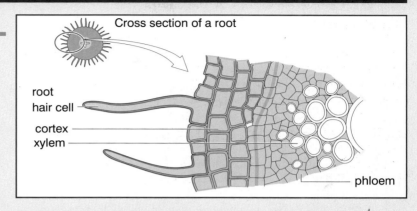

Cross section of a root

root hair cell

cortex

xylem

phloem

Adaptation

How this makes the cell better at its job

long hair-like structure that comes out from the cell body

increases the surface area and allows the uptake of water and minerals to take place quicker

no waxy layer outside the cell

allows for quicker uptake of water

no chloroplasts

not needed because there is no light for photosynthesis in the soil

Palisade cell (plant)

Function

To enable photosynthesis to be carried out efficiently.

Cell structure and adaptations

The palisade cell is found in the upper part of the leaf, as shown in the diagram opposite.

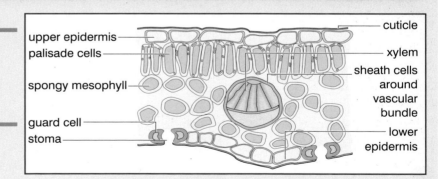

cuticle

upper epidermis

palisade cells

xylem

sheath cells around vascular bundle

spongy mesophyll

guard cell

stoma

lower epidermis

Adaptation

How this makes the cell better at its job

lots of chloroplasts

allows more photosynthesis to take place

chloroplasts are arranged in the cell so that they are nearer to the leaf surface

chloroplasts are exposed to a high light intensity

CHECK YOURSELF QUESTIONS

Q1 Why are there many different types of cell?

Q2 Complete the labels on the diagram of a sperm cell below. Explain how a sperm cell is well adapted to its function.

Q3 Describe two ways in which root hair cells and palisade cells are adapted to fulfil their particular functions.

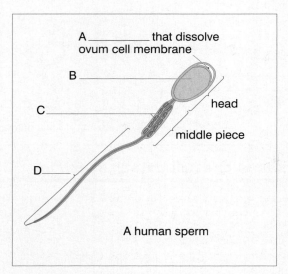

A _____ that dissolve
ovum cell membrane

B _____

C _____

D _____

head

middle piece

A human sperm

Respiration

What you should already know

- The appropriate scientific terminology to use when describing life processes such as respiration.

- How to use word equations to summarise chemical reactions.

WHAT YOU NEED TO KNOW

LIVING ORGANISMS AND ENERGY

- All living organisms need energy. Animals need energy for the following reasons:
  - so that they can move about;
  - for growth;
  - to make specialised cells for reproduction;
  - in some cases, to keep their body at a constant temperature.

- Plants need energy for the following reasons:
  - to make their (slow) movements;
  - for growth;
  - to make specialised reproductive cells;
  - to take minerals up from the soil.

- Organisms get their energy from food. Getting energy from food is called **respiration**. All living things do this, and we say that they **respire**. Animals eat other animals or plants to get their food. Plants produce the carbohydrate needed for respiration during the process of photosynthesis (see Unit 2, Revision Session 4).

- Food is a store of chemical energy. Different types of food have different amounts of energy stored inside them.

1 g fat gives about	38 kJ of energy
1 g carbohydrate (sugars and starch) gives about	17 kJ of energy
1 g protein gives about	17 kJ of energy

fat   carbohydrate   protein

- Proteins are not usually used to provide energy. Living organisms normally use carbohydrates to provide energy because it is easier to release energy from carbohydrates than proteins. Living things also use fat, which contains more energy per gram than either of the other two types of food.

GETTING ENERGY FROM FOOD

- Respiration takes place inside living cells. It happens inside tiny specialised parts of the cell called **mitochondria** (see Revision Session 3, *Specialised Cells*). The food is usually made to react with oxygen, releasing energy and some waste substances. The waste materials are carbon dioxide and water.

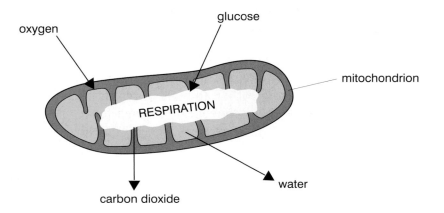

- Mitochondria carry out respiration most efficiently when food is in the form of glucose, so foods are normally changed into glucose before the cell uses them in respiration. This type of respiration is called **aerobic respiration**, because it uses oxygen from the air. We can write a word equation to summarise aerobic respiration:

energy is released
glucose + oxygen ⟶ carbon dioxide + water

The full chemical symbol equation is:

$$C_6H_{12}O_6 + 6O_2 \xrightarrow{\text{energy is released}} 6CO_2 + 6H_2O$$

- Aerobic respiration is an example of an **oxidation reaction**. The cell oxidises glucose producing carbon dioxide and water whilst releasing energy.

- To get oxygen to their cells, many animals breathe air into their lungs. The blood then carries oxygen from the lungs to the living cells.

- The digestive system breaks down food and the intestines absorb the digested food into the blood. The blood then carries digested food to the cells. It is the blood that brings the oxygen and glucose to the cells so that respiration can take place.

? CHECK YOURSELF QUESTIONS

Q1 What is respiration?

Q2 Copy and complete this paragraph:

Animals need energy to m .... , for g .... and for r .... Some animals use energy to keep their body at a constant t .... Plants need energy for g .... , r .... and for taking up some m .... from the soil.

Q3 Write down the word equation for aerobic respiration.

Human Impact on the Environment

> **What you should already know**
>
> - The environment in which animals and plants live is called a habitat.
>
> - The organisms in a particular habitat are all linked in food chains and food webs.
>
> - The number of organisms at each level of a food chain can be represented in a pyramid of numbers.

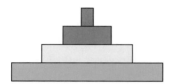

WHAT YOU NEED TO KNOW

- At each level in the food chain there are usually fewer organisms than in the level below. This can be shown in a pyramid of numbers (see page 96).

- This means that each of the primary consumers eats a number of producers and each secondary consumer eats a number of primary consumers.

- If a producer is treated with a herbicide or a primary consumer population is treated with a pesticide, then this has effects on animals higher up the food chain. For example, if a gardener puts slug pellets on a flower bed then these will be eaten by the slugs. However, if a blackbird then eats several slugs the blackbird in turn will be poisoned. The dose of poison that the blackbird receives will be magnified by the number of slugs that it eats.

  plants → slugs → blackbirds

- Human activity can also affect food chains and webs in other ways. Consider this woodland food web.

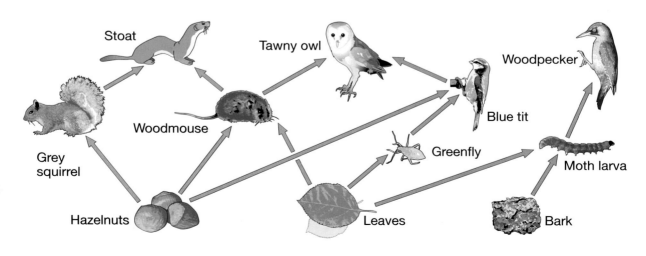

- If a gardener living near this wood sprays his roses to kill the greenfly, then the total greenfly population in the area will go down. This will mean that:

  - The blue tits will have less greenfly to eat so the population may go down.
  - The tawny owls will then have fewer blue tits to eat so the population may also go down.
  - The blue tits may compete more with the woodmice and grey squirrels for the hazelnuts – so the populations of woodmice and grey squirrels may go down. This might further reduce the population of tawny owls.
  - If the tawny owl population has gone down, then there may be more woodmice to compete for fewer hazelnuts – because some of them are being eaten by the blue tits. If the woodmice and grey squirrel populations are affected, then the stoats will be affected too!

CHECK YOURSELF QUESTIONS

Look at this food chain for a woodland habitat.

oak tree → caterpillars → great tits → sparrowhawks

Q1 Draw a pyramid of numbers for this food chain.

A pesticide was sprayed onto a field near this habitat. The wind blew some of the pesticide into the wood. The pesticide did not affect the trees, the caterpillars or the tits but the sparrowhawks began to die.

Q2 Explain why this happened.

> **What you should already know**
>
> - Matter is made up of particles.
> - Elements consist of atoms.
> - Some elements combine through chemical reactions to form compounds.

WHAT YOU NEED TO KNOW

- Chemical elements can be represented by symbols and chemical compounds can be represented by formulae. There are 92 naturally occurring elements and more than a dozen other elements that have been made in laboratories. Each element has its own symbol which is a shorter way of writing its name. The periodic table shows all of the elements that exist, using the symbol to represent each one. The periodic table is organised so that the elements belonging to 'chemical families' are shown close to each other. Elements in families have some properties in common.

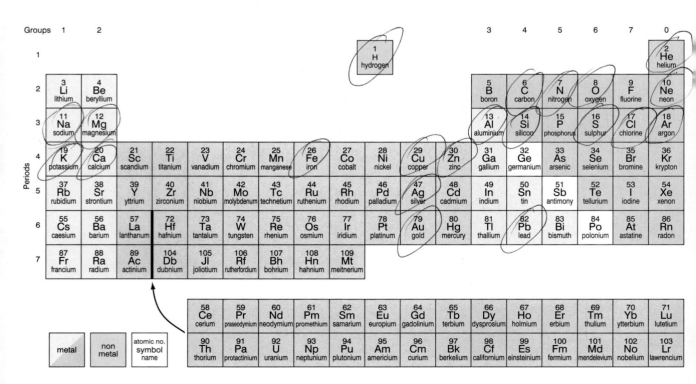

- You do not need to know the symbols of all of the elements in the periodic table but you need to be familiar with the symbols of the most common elements. This table gives the names and symbols for the elements that you are likely to come across in Key Stage 3.

Metals		Non-metals	
Name	**Symbol**	**Name**	**Symbol**
sodium	Na	hydrogen	H
magnesium	Mg	helium	He
aluminium	Al	carbon	C
potassium	K	nitrogen	N
calcium	Ca	oxygen	O
iron	Fe	neon	Ne
copper	Cu	silicon	Si
zinc	Zn	sulphur	S
silver	Ag	chlorine	Cl
gold	Au	argon	Ar
lead	Pb		

WRITING CHEMICAL FORMULAE

- When two or more atoms are joined together by chemical bonds they form a **molecule**. A molecule can be formed by a combination of different elements or by a combination of the same type of atom. A **formula** states what elements are present in the molecule and how many of each there are.

- The formula that most people learn first is that of water, H_2O. This tells you it contains the elements hydrogen H and oxygen O and that there are two hydrogen atoms for every one oxygen atom. The number of atoms of each type is given by the small number that follows it, so H for hydrogen followed by a 2 tells us that there are two hydrogen atoms. The oxygen does not have a number after it so there is only one atom present. No other element is written in the formula, so the molecule only contains these two elements.

- The formula for sodium chloride is NaCl. This means that for every sodium atom present, there is one chlorine atom present.

The table below gives some more examples. If there is a metal atom in the compound, it is usually the first symbol to be written.

Formula	Elements	Name
$MgCl_2$	Mg × 1 ; Cl × 2	magnesium chloride
Na_2O	Na × 2 ; O × 1	sodium oxide
Al_2O_3	Al × 2 ; O × 3	aluminium oxide
$CuSO_4$	Cu × 1 ; S × 1 ; O × 4	copper sulphate
Cl_2	Cl × 2	chlorine (molecule)

- Sometimes a bracket is used in a formula. This means that everything inside the bracket is multiplied by the number to the right of the bracket. This is shown by the formula for calcium hydroxide, $Ca(OH)_2$. It shows that for every calcium atom, two oxygen atoms and two hydrogen atoms are present. Another example is aluminium hydroxide, $Al(OH)_3$. For every aluminium atom, there are three oxygen atoms and three hydrogen atoms.

- If there are numbers inside and outside the bracket you just follow both rules – you must multiply the number of each type of atom inside the brackets by the number outside the brackets to get the total number of each atom. For example, $Ca(NO_3)_2$ contains one calcium atom for every two nitrogen atoms and six oxygen atoms.

- Acids are important chemical compounds and they all contain hydrogen. The three most common laboratory acids are:

  hydrochloric acid   HCl
  sulphuric acid H_2SO_4
  nitric acid HNO_3

- Acids react with bases, which are oxides or hydroxides. Two examples of bases are:

  copper oxide   CuO
  sodium hydroxide   NaOH

- Acids will also react with carbonates. All carbonates contain the CO_3 group. Two examples are:

  potassium carbonate K_2CO_3
  calcium carbonate $CaCO_3$

- A formula for a molecule shows that it has a fixed number of each atom that makes up the compound. The formula never changes even if you make the compound in different ways. You can make copper oxide by heating copper carbonate, or you can make it by heating copper in oxygen. It has the formula CuO no matter which method is used to produce it.

CHECK YOURSELF QUESTIONS

Q1 Construct a table and sort these substances into either elements or compounds:

Na O_2 NaCl $Ca(OH)_2$ Al Al_2O_3
H_2O N_2 H_2SO_4 HCl   Ne

Q2 Write the correct chemical formulae for the following:

a water, a molecule that contains 2 hydrogen atoms for every 1 oxygen atom;

b sulphuric acid, which contains 2 hydrogen atoms for every 1 sulphur atom and 4 oxygen atoms.

c sodium carbonate, which contains 2 sodium atoms for every 1 carbon atom and 3 oxygen atoms;

d calcium hydroxide, which contains 1 calcium atom for every 2 pairs of 1 oxygen and 1 hydrogen;

e ethane, a molecule that contains 2 carbon atoms and 6 hydrogen atoms.

Q3 How many atoms of each element are there in the formulae of the following compounds?

a SO_2

b Fe_2O_3

c CH_4

d $Zn(NO_3)_2$

e $(NH_4)_2SO_4$

Weathering

> **What you should already know**
>
> - There are similarities between some chemical reactions.
> - Changes of state are related to energy transfers.
> - Materials expand and contract with changes in temperature.

WHAT YOU NEED TO KNOW

- Weathering is the process by which rocks on the surface of the Earth are broken down by the action of 'atmospheric agents'. Some of the agents are **physical**, such as the effect of frost damage. Other agents are **chemical**, such as the effect of a weak acid on some kinds of rocks.

PHYSICAL WEATHERING OF ROCKS

- **Physical weathering** is the process that breaks down larger pieces of rock into smaller ones, eventually leading to the formation of sediment. Expansion and contraction play an important part in the physical weathering of rocks. Rocks in very hot places such as deserts can be weathered by the repeated expansion and contraction of the rock. This happens because of the extreme changes in temperature between day and night. Rocks that have expanded during the day because of the high temperatures experience a large and sudden drop in temperature when the Sun goes down. The resulting rapid contraction creates forces in the rock which lead to it fracturing and breaking up. This happens every day, causing the rocks to break down into smaller and smaller pieces.

- Most materials contract when they change from a liquid to a solid. Water is an exception. The expansion of water causes weathering of rocks. Just around its freezing point, as it forms ice, water expands. If water seeps into a crack in a rock and then freezes, the force of it expanding is so great that it can make the crack in the rock wider. If this keeps happening, part of the rock will break away.

a)
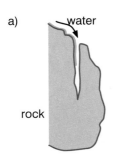
water

rock

Water runs into the crack

b)
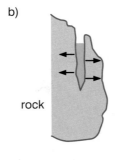
rock

Water freezes
in the crack
and expands

c)
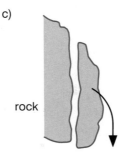
rock

The forces produced
crack the rock and
the piece breaks away

CHEMICAL WEATHERING OF ROCKS

- **Chemical weathering** is the process where chemicals in the air react with a mineral in a rock. The process happens with acidic solutions and is usually associated with rainwater. All rain is slightly acidic because it dissolves carbon dioxide from the atmosphere (forming carbonic acid). This slightly acidic solution reacts with the calcium carbonate (the main component of limestone, chalk or marble) and produces calcium hydrogencarbonate:

  limestone + water + carbon dioxide → calcium hydrogencarbonate
  $$CaCO_3 + H_2O + CO_2 \rightarrow Ca(HCO_3)_2$$

- Calcium hydrogencarbonate is soluble in water, so the rock is gradually dissolved away.

- When rain falls on areas of limestone rock the reaction leads to the formation of underground caverns. Stalagmites and stalactites, like those shown below, are formed when calcium hydrogencarbonate decomposes into insoluble calcium carbonate, carbon dioxide and water.

- Burning fossil fuels such as coal increases the amount of carbon dioxide in the atmosphere. In addition, impurities in the fuel lead to the production of compounds in the air such as sulphur dioxide gas. When this gas dissolves in rainwater, it forms a much stronger acid (sulphuric acid) and this is what is called 'acid rain'. The reactions of 'acid rain' with all types of rocks are much more vigorous than the effect of slightly acidic rainwater on limestone. Rocks such as limestone, chalk and marble dissolve much faster, causing serious problems to buildings in areas where there is a high level of atmospheric pollution. Acid rain can also lead to the corrosion of metals.

? CHECK YOURSELF QUESTIONS

Q1 Describe two ways in which rock can be weathered by physical processes.

Q2 Limestone is a useful source of building stone, but it is affected by chemical weathering. Explain why this is a more serious problem in a city than in the countryside.

Reactivity Series

> **What you should already know**
>
> - Metals react with oxygen to form oxides.
> - Metals react with acids and produce hydrogen.
> - Different metals react at different rates with the same reactants.

WHAT YOU NEED TO KNOW

- Some metals are very reactive and will tarnish (lose their shine) in a few seconds when exposed to the air. The metal sodium does this. Some metals, however, such as copper and silver take a long time to tarnish when left in the same conditions. The tarnishing process occurs when the metal reacts with oxygen and forms a layer of metal oxide on the surface. It is possible to carry out a series of experiments by cleaning the surfaces of several common metals and exposing them to air. By measuring the time taken for each one to tarnish, the metals can be ranked in order of how quickly they react with oxygen in air. This gives a simple comparison of how reactive each metal is in relation to the others. This is known as a **trend in reactivity**.

- Results from a wide range of chemical experiments have shown that all metals can be put into a list in the order of their reactivity. This list is called the **reactivity series**.

Sodium (top) reacts very quickly with oxygen in the air; copper reacts very slowly. Sodium is more reative than copper.

Most reactive	potassium	K		
	sodium	Na		
	calcium	Ca		
	magnesium	Mg		
	aluminium	Al		
	carbon	C		
	zinc	Zn		increasing
	iron	Fe		reactivity
	tin	Sn		
	lead	Pb		
	hydrogen	H		
	copper	Cu		
	silver	Ag		
Least reactive	gold	Au		

- This list shows the order of reactivity for the most common metals. It also includes the non-metals hydrogen and carbon because they both take part in reactions with some metals and not with others. With sufficient information, all other metals could be added to this list in the appropriate position.

- We can use the reactivity series to predict what will happen in particular chemical reactions. The most reactive metal in the series is potassium. Potassium reacts violently with cold water to produce hydrogen so rapidly that it bursts into flames.

$$2K + 2H_2O \rightarrow 2KOH + H_2$$

- Calcium is lower down the series, so it reacts less violently than potassium with cold water. Calcium reacts with cold water, producing a steady stream of hydrogen gas. Because of their relative positions in the reactivity series, it is possible to predict that the reaction of sodium with cold water will be quite vigorous and that the reaction of magnesium with cold water will be slower than that of calcium. This is actually the case. To get magnesium to react quickly with water it has to be heated in the presence of steam instead of cold water. The pattern in these reactions is that all the metals that do react produce hydrogen gas.

- The trend in the reactions is that the higher a metal is in the reactivity series, the more vigorous its reaction is with cold water. Knowing this makes it reasonable to predict that copper will not react with cold water because of its position in the reactivity series. None of the metals lower than hydrogen will produce hydrogen in any reaction. Copper will not react with water under any conditions and that is one good reason why we can use copper for water pipes in our homes.

PREDICTING THE REACTIONS OF METALS

- The metals follow the same order of reactivity for all their reactions, so now we can make predictions for the reactions of metals with other substances. We said in Unit 2, Revision Session 8, *Chemical Reactions* that metals react with acids and produce hydrogen. For example:

$$Mg + H_2SO_4 \rightarrow MgSO_4 + H_2$$

- We cannot try potassium and sodium because their reactions with acids would be too dangerous. Even calcium is very reactive with very dilute acids, but metals like zinc and iron both react steadily. The metals at the lower end of the reactivity series do not react with diluted acids at all. Using the reactivity series, we can predict that magnesium will react with an acid faster than zinc, but more slowly than calcium. Again, this is what happens.

DISPLACEMENT REACTIONS

- The reaction of a metal with an acid is an example from a range of reactions called **displacement reactions**. All acids contain hydrogen and in a metal–acid reaction, the metal displaces the hydrogen from the acid. If a metal is high in the reactivity series, it will displace any element which is lower in the series. For example, magnesium displaces hydrogen from acid – hydrogen is released because it has been displaced. Copper is lower than hydrogen so it cannot displace it and copper will never react to produce hydrogen.

- A metal can displace another metal from one of its compounds in solution. For example, if a piece of iron is dipped into a solution of copper sulphate for about a minute and is then removed, it emerges from the solution coated with a thin layer of pure copper metal. This happens because iron is higher in the reactivity series than copper. Iron is more reactive so it forms compounds more readily than copper. Because some of the iron forms a compound, some of the copper must be removed from the compound – it is displaced. The copper becomes a metal and the iron forms a compound.

- A metal that is higher in the reactivity series than another metal will displace the metal that is below it in the series.

- We can use the difference in reactivity to make predictions about what might happen in some chemical reactions. It is reasonable to predict that:
  - iron will displace lead from lead nitrate solution;
  - copper will not displace magnesium from magnesium sulphate solution;
  - calcium will displace zinc from zinc sulphate solution.

- However, these are only predictions based on a knowledge of the reactivity series and they do not tell you anything about the reaction itself.

CHECK YOURSELF QUESTIONS

Use the reactivity series on page 115 to answer these questions.

Q1 Name two metals that are about as reactive as calcium.

Q2 Name two metals that are about as reactive as iron.

Q3 Which two metals are likely to be found in the ground in their pure form uncombined with any other elements?

Q4 In which of the following cases can a displacement reaction take place? Name the metals that are displaced.

a $Mg + CuSO_4$

b $Fe + MgSO_4$

c $Cu + Pb(NO_3)_2$

d $Zn + Ag(NO_3)_2$

e $Mg + FeSO_4$

Environmental Chemistry

> **What you should already know**
>
> • Human actions can have an effect on other species.

WHAT YOU NEED TO KNOW

- The effects of pesticides and herbicides, (see page 106), are not the only impacts that humans have on the environment.

- Burning fossil fuels produces **sulphur dioxide** which can cause **acid rain**. This damages buildings and metals, and can also change the acidity of lakes. This in turn can affect the plants and animals in that habitat. The acidity can be neutralised by adding limestone to the lake. Acid rain can also have a direct effect on trees and plants.

Neutralising the acidity of a lake in Sweden

Trees affected by acid rain

- The **carbon dioxide** produced by burning fossil fuels goes up into the atmosphere and forms an insulating layer. The heat from the Sun can get through this layer but the reflected heat that bounces back from the Earth's surface gets trapped in the upper atmosphere. This is called the **greenhouse effect** and the increase in this effect is the cause of **global warming**. If global warming continues, then the polar ice caps may melt and sea levels will rise. Our climate may become more extreme with gales and hurricanes becoming more common and some places becoming very dry, while others may experience much higher levels of rainfall.

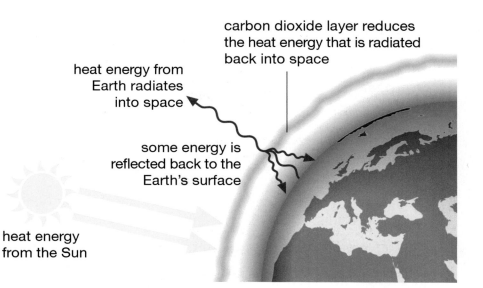

carbon dioxide layer reduces the heat energy that is radiated back into space

heat energy from Earth radiates into space

some energy is reflected back to the Earth's surface

heat energy from the Sun

CHECK YOURSELF QUESTIONS

Q1 Which chemical that is produced by burning fossil fuels contributes to:

a acid rain;

b global warming?

Q2 Give three possible effects of global warming.

a ....

b ....

c ....

> **What you should already know**
>
> - When white light passes through a coloured filter, the colour of light leaving the filter is the same as the colour of the filter.
>
> - A glass prism can be used to split up (disperse) white light into a spectrum.
>
> - The three primary colours of light are red, green and blue.
>
> - Objects appear black because no light is reflected from them.

Mixing light

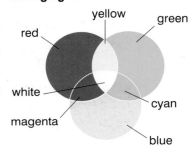

WHAT YOU NEED TO KNOW

- If three spotlights, each producing one of the primary colours of light, are shone onto a screen so that the areas of light overlap, then the screen will be lit with the colours shown on the left.

- When two or more primary colours of light are added together they produce what is called a **secondary colour**. Cyan, magenta, yellow and white are all secondary colours of light. We can represent these combinations of colours in the following way:

red + green = yellow

green + blue = cyan

red + blue = magenta

red + blue + green = white

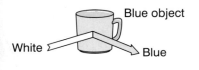

- When white light shines onto a blue object it looks blue. A blue object will reflect blue light. All of the other colours are absorbed.

- If red light shines onto a white object, the object will look red. A white object reflects all of the light shining onto it.

- A black object does not reflect any light, so no matter what colour light shines onto it, it will always look black. Black **absorbs** all colours.

- When red light shines onto a blue object, it looks black. There is no blue light for the object to reflect, and the red light is absorbed.

- But what happens if we shine coloured lights onto secondary colours? Look again at the chart showing what secondary colours are made up of and then look at the following combinations of coloured objects being illuminated by different colours of light.

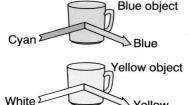

- If cyan light (made from blue and green light) shines onto a blue object, the blue light is reflected and the green light is absorbed, so the object will look blue.

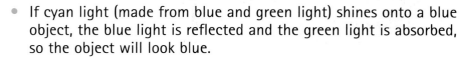

- A yellow object will reflect red and green light. It will look yellow when white light shines on it.

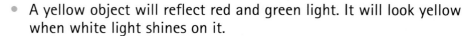

- If red light shines onto a yellow object, red light is reflected, so the object looks red.

- If blue light shines onto a yellow object it will look black because no light is reflected.

- If green light shines onto a yellow object, green light is reflected.

- Many objects are coloured using dyes that are not pure colours so if you shine different colours of light onto them they may not reflect light the way you might expect.

CHECK YOURSELF QUESTIONS

Q1 A sheet of white paper has red crosses on it. What will be seen when the paper is illuminated by:

a red light;

b magenta light?

Q2 Misha's costume for a school play consists of a red hat, a green jacket, a white scarf and magenta trousers. White, blue, yellow and red spotlights are used on the stage. Complete the table to show what colours Misha's costume will appear under the different coloured spotlights.

	White light	Blue light	Yellow light	Red light
Red hat				
Green jacket	green	black	green	black
White scarf				
Magenta trousers				

Moments and Turning Forces

> **What you should already know**
>
> • Unbalanced forces can make objects change shape, speed or direction.

WHAT YOU SHOULD KNOW

- Turning forces only cause an object to turn when they are not balanced. If an object has equal and opposite turning forces it will not move. We say it is in **equilibrium**.

- We can usually assume that for a straight beam, like a ladder, its own weight acts at the centre which is why it will balance if supported in the middle.

- The size of a turning force will depend on two things – the size of the force and the distance from the pivot.

  Look at this diagram:

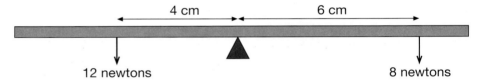

- On the left-hand side there is 12 newtons of force acting 4 cm from the pivot.

- This gives a moment or turning force of 12 N x 4 cm = 48 N cm. This is acting in an anticlockwise direction.

- On the right-hand side there is 8 newtons of force acting 6 cm from the pivot.

- This gives a moment or turning force of 8 N x 6 cm = 48 N cm. This is acting in a clockwise direction.

- Because the anticlockwise and clockwise moments are both 48 N cm, the beam is balanced. If either of the weights were moved, then the beam would become unbalanced even though the size of the weights had not changed.

- We make use of turning forces in lots of ways. A long handle makes it possible to exert a bigger turning force for a smaller effort. This is how spanners and pump handles work – and part of the reason it is easier to use a suitcase with wheels at one corner than if you just tried to carry the same thing!

? CHECK YOURSELF QUESTIONS

Q1 If you want to hang a ladder on a single hook so that it balances horizontally:

a where should the hook be placed?

b why?

Q2 Look at the beam below and explain what would have to be done to weight A to make it balance.

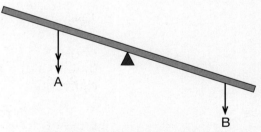

	Weight	Distance from pivot
A	6 N	5 cm
B	3 N	14 cm

> **What you should already know**
>
> - Surface area is measured in square metres (m²) or square centimetres (cm²).
> - Objects have weight caused by gravitational attraction.
> - Weight is a force and is measured in newtons (N).

WHAT YOU NEED TO KNOW

- It is easier to cut an onion with a sharp knife than with a blunt knife. When the knife's blade is sharp, the surface area of blade that is in contact with the onion is smaller. Even though the force you apply with each knife blade may be the same, the smaller surface area of the sharp blade means you can apply greater **pressure**.

- The pressure applied to a surface will increase if:
  - the applied force increases;
  - the area over which the force is applied decreases.

- If a person tries to walk on deep snow wearing shoes, they will sink further into the snow than someone wearing skis. When a person wears skis, their weight is spread over a larger area than for someone wearing shoes. Therefore, the pressure is low and they can move easily over the top of the snow. When a person wears shoes, their weight is spread over a much smaller area. The pressure is higher and their feet drop down through the snow as they walk.

- Pressure is the force acting **normally** (at right angles) on each unit area of a particular surface. It is calculated by using the expression:

$$\text{pressure} = \frac{\text{force}}{\text{area}}$$

- If the force is measured in newtons (N) and the area is in square metres (m²) then the pressure is measured in N/m². This unit (newton per square metre) is also called the pascal (Pa). If the area is measured in square centimetres (cm²), the pressure is measured in N/cm².

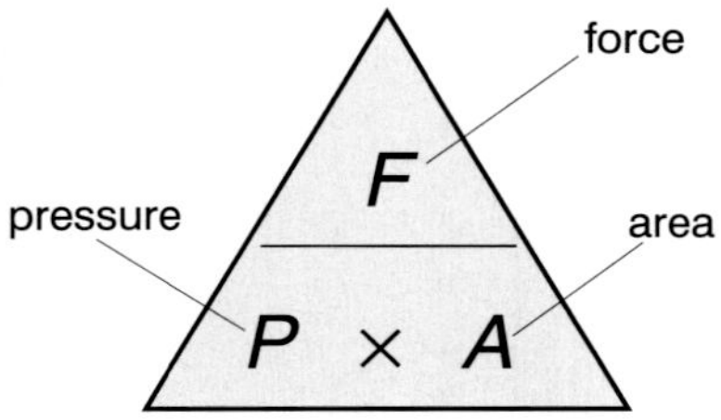

The triangle shown on the left can be used to help answer problems about pressure. First, cover up the part you need to find. Then read off the equation you need to use.

- For example, to find force, cover the letter *F* with your finger. The letters that remain show you how to calculate the force.

  force = pressure x area

- To find area, cover the letter *A* with your finger. Now, read off what remains:

  $$\text{area} = \frac{\text{force}}{\text{pressure}}$$

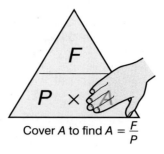

Cover *A* to find $A = \frac{F}{P}$

Cover *F* to find *F = P x A*

- To find pressure, cover the letter *P* with your finger and what is left shows you how to calculate pressure:

  $$\text{pressure} = \frac{\text{force}}{\text{area}}$$

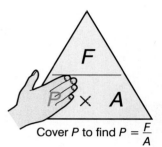

Cover *P* to find $P = \frac{F}{A}$

EXAMPLES OF CALCULATING PRESSURE
- Consider a paving slab that is 40 cm long, 50 cm wide, 5 cm deep and weighs 200 N.

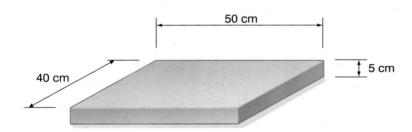

50 cm

40 cm

5 cm

- There are three different ways of storing this size of slab, each with a different surface in contact with the ground:

  a   flat on a 40 cm x 50 cm face   (surface area = 40 cm x 50 cm = 2000 cm²)

  b   on its longer side, 50 cm x 5 cm   (surface area = 50 cm x 5 cm = 250 cm²)

  c   on its shorter side, 40 cm x 5 cm   (surface area = 40 cm x 5 cm = 200 cm²)

- The pressure applied to the ground in each of these situations is different:

In **a**, pressure = $\dfrac{\text{force}}{\text{area}} = \dfrac{200\text{ N}}{2000\text{ cm}^2}$ = 0.1 N/cm²

In **b**, pressure = $\dfrac{\text{force}}{\text{area}} = \dfrac{200\text{ N}}{250\text{ cm}^2}$ = 0.8 N/cm²

In **c**, pressure = $\dfrac{\text{force}}{\text{area}} = \dfrac{200\text{ N}}{200\text{ cm}^2}$ = 1 N/cm²

- The smaller the area of slab in contact with the ground, the higher the pressure it exerts.

CHECK YOURSELF QUESTIONS

Q1 What pressure is applied to the ground when a box which has a weight of 300N stands on an end that has an area of 6m²?

Q2 Why does a tractor have very wide tyres?

Q3

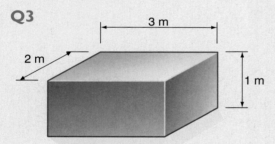

The above box weighs 30 N and is to be placed onto some sand.

a What is the largest pressure it could exert on the sand?

b What is the smallest pressure it could exert on the sand?

c Will the box sink further into the sand when it is placed as in (a) or as in (b)?

Q4

Chris and his snowboard weigh a total of 600 N.

The snow board has an area of 3000 cm².

a What is the total force exerted on the snow by Chris and his snowboard?

b Calculate the pressure exerted by the snowboard on the snow when the snowboard is flat. Give the unit.

c When Chris carries his snowboard, his pressure on the snow is six times greater than when he is snow boarding. Explain why.

> **What you should already know**
>
> - Magnetic fields are regions of space where magnetic materials experience forces of magnetic attraction.
>
> - The shape of the magnetic field pattern produced by a bar magnet.
>
> - An electric current is a flow of charge around an electrical circuit.

WHAT YOU NEED TO KNOW

- When an electrical current flows through a wire, a magnetic field is produced around the wire. This can be demonstrated by passing a single wire, at right angles, through a horizontal piece of card. With the current switched on, iron filings are spread across the card. By tapping the card gently, the shape of the magnetic field produced becomes visible (as shown on the right).

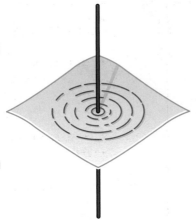

- When an electric current flows through a coil of wire, the weak magnetic field can be concentrated so that the coil behaves like a bar magnet. The magnetic field around the coil can be represented by the pattern shown in the diagram below.

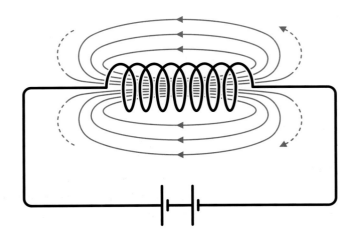

- If the current flowing in the coil is reversed, the direction of the magnetic field is also reversed.

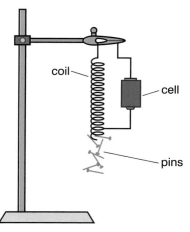

- When this current is switched on, the coil can be used to pick up small objects such as pins. The number of pins the coil picks up depends on its strength. The magnetic effect of the coil can be increased by:
  - making more turns in the coil;
  - increasing the size of the current flowing through the coil;
  - placing an iron core inside the coil.

- Increasing the number of turns in the coil increases the number of sections of wire. The field around each of the turns contributes to the total magnetic effect of the coil.

- Increasing the size of the current through the coil increases the strength of the magnetic field around each length of the coil wire. Placing an iron core inside the coil concentrates the magnetic field into this magnetic material, increasing the overall magnetic effect of the coil.

- All commercial electromagnets have a soft iron core. Soft iron is magnetic but, unlike steel, does not become permanently magnetised when surrounded by the coil of the electromagnet. Using soft iron makes it possible to switch the electromagnet off.

- Electromagnets have many different uses. The current can be adjusted to change the strength (or attractive force) of the magnet. They can be used in electric bells and relays. A relay is a switch that uses a small change in current to control another circuit. Doctors can use electromagnets to remove steel splinters from a person's eye. Another use is in circuit breakers.

A CIRCUIT BREAKER USING AN ELECTROMAGNET

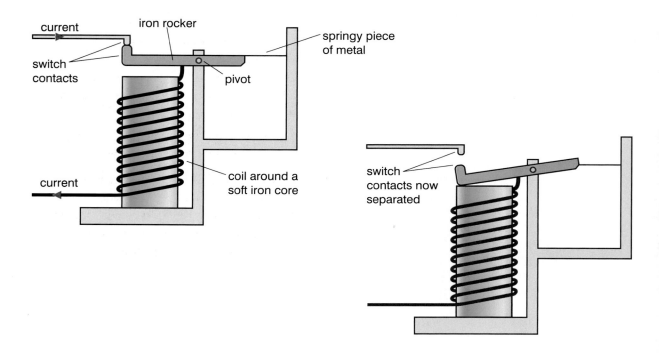

- A circuit breaker is a safety switch that opens when the current in a circuit becomes too large. Look at the diagram on the previous page.

1 The springy piece of metal holds the iron rocker in place so that the switch contacts are together.

2 The coil becomes an electromagnet when a current passes through it.

3 If the current becomes too large, the electromagnet becomes strong enough to overcome the force of the springy piece of metal, and the left-hand side of the iron rocker moves down towards the coil.

4 The switch contacts open and the current can no longer flow, so the components in the circuit are protected.

CHECK YOURSELF QUESTIONS

Q1 The diagram shows a simple coil. Give three ways in which this coil could be made into a stronger electromagnet.

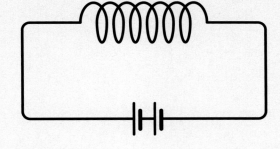

Q2

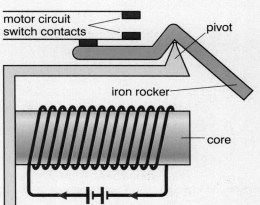

The diagram shows an electromagnetic relay. It is a switch that is used to turn on a large current using a small current.

Write the following sentences in the correct order to explain how the relay works:

- The iron rocker is attracted to the coil.
- The switch contacts are closed.
- An electric current flows through the coil.
- A current flows in the motor circuit.
- The coil becomes magnetised.

I   **a**   Scientists studied the animals and plants in a large wood, over a period of time. One food chain in the wood is show below.

Oak trees → winter moth caterpillars → great tits → sparrowhawks

Draw a pyramid of numbers for this food chain.   *(2 marks)*

b   Insecticide was sprayed onto fields near the wood. Some of the insecticide was blown into the wood by the wind.

(i) In the food chain above, the sparrowhawks contained the highest concentration of insecticide. Explain why.

....

....   *(2 marks)*

(ii) The use of insecticides could cause the population of sparrowhawks to decrease.

Give **one** other reason why the population of sparrowhawks might decrease.

....   *(1 mark)*

c   The graph shows how the number of pairs of great tits changed in the wood over a period of time.

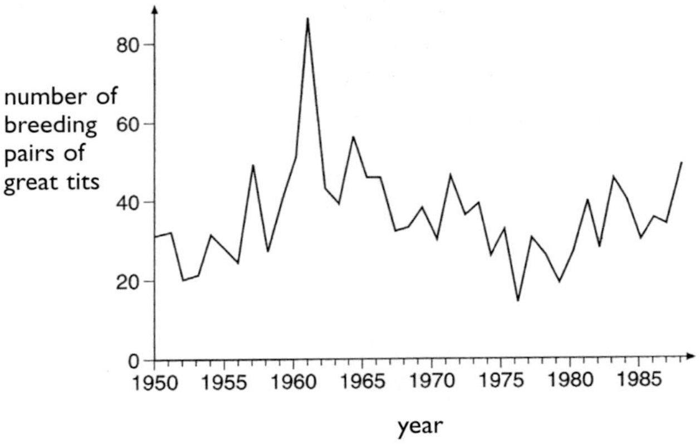

(i) Use the graph to suggest the year when there were probably fewest sparrowhawks in the wood.

....

What is the evidence from the graph for your answer?

....

....   *(1 mark)*

(ii) Explain the reasoning for the answer you have given in part c(i).

....

....   *(1 mark)*

maximum 7 marks

2 In the eighteenth century, scientists had different ideas about what happens when metals burn in air.

Priestley

When metals burn in air, they **lose** something to the air and a powder is formed.

When metals burn in air, they **gain** something from the air and a powder is formed.

Lavoisier

a Imagine you want to investigate the ideas of Priestley and Lavoisier.
Assume you have been given three pieces of different metals.
In a laboratory, metals are heated to high temperatures in crucibles.
You would also have access to all the usual laboratory equipment.

lid
crucible

In your plan you must give:
- the **one** factor you would change as you carry out your investigation (the independent variable);
- **one** factor you would observe or measure to collect your results (the dependent variable);
- **one** of the factors you would keep the same as you carry out your investigation;
- the **evidence** that would support Lavoisier's idea.

.... (*1 mark*)

.... (*1 mark*)

.... (*1 mark*)

.... (*1 mark*)

b In the box below, draw and label a table you could use to record your results.

(*1 mark*)

maximum 5 marks

3 The diagram shows a candle burning in air under a bell-jar.

a (i) When the candle burns, there is a reaction. Give the chemical formulae of the products of this reaction.

1 ....

2 ....

(2 marks)

Bell-jar

air-tight seal

candle

sheet of glass

(ii) As the candle burns, some of the candle wax is used up. Give **two** other observations which would show that a chemical reaction is taking place.

1..

....

2...

....

(2 marks)

b A potted plant is placed under a bell-jar as shown here.

Photosynthesis in the leaves causes changes in the proportion of the gases in the bell-jar.

plant

clear plastic bag tied tightly around the plant pot

Bell-jar

air-tight seal

sheet of glass

(i) In bright sunlight, what are **two** of these changes?

1 ....

2 ....

(2 marks)

(ii) Explain why the changes will be different if the plant is kept in the dark.

....

....

....

(2 marks)

c Chlorophyll is the green substance present in cells in the leaves.

(i) Give the name of the part of the cell which contains chlorophyll.

....

(1 mark)

(ii) Which part of the cell controls the production of chlorophyll?

....

(1 mark)

maximum 10 marks

4 Railway lines can be joined together by pouring molten iron into the gap between them.

a The molten iron is produced by the reaction between powdered aluminium and iron oxide. Complete the word equation for the reaction.

Aluminium + iron oxide → iron + ... *(1 mark)*

b Iron can be produced from a mixture of aluminium and iron oxide but **not** from a mixture of copper and iron oxide.
Write the names of the **three** metals, in the order of their reactivity.

most reactive ....

....

.... *(1 mark)*

c The list shows the names and symbols of five metals in order of their reactivity.

name	symbol
sodium	Na
calcium	Ca
magnesium	Mg
zinc	Zn
silver	Ag

(i) What, if anything, would be the result of heating zinc powder with calcium oxide?

.... *(1 mark)*

(ii) Write down the **name** of a metal in the list that will **not** react with a solution of magnesium sulphate.

.... *(1 mark)*

d The powdered metal with the symbol Zn burns in air.
Write the **word equation** for the reaction.

.... *(2 marks)*

maximum 6 marks

5 A headline from a newspaper is shown below.

British Power
Stations cause
Acid Rain in
Scandinavia

Some countries claim that acid rain caused by power stations in Britain damages their forests. Others argue that coal-burning power stations produce cheap electricity and that plants can stand some level of acid rain.

Imagine you are planning a laboratory investigation of the claim:
'**plants can stand some level of acid rain**'.

Assume you have access to whatever laboratory equipment you need, including:
• seeds   • acid   • seed trays   • soil

Plan a laboratory investigation to test the claim that *'plants can stand some level of acid rain'*.

a   Name a factor you would need to vary in your investigation. (This is the independent variable.)

....
(1 mark)

b   (i) What factor would you examine to see the effect? (This is the dependent variable.)

....
(1 mark)

(ii) How could you measure this dependent variable?

....
(1 mark)

c   Suggest **one** factor you would control to ensure that your investigation is fair.

....
(1 mark)

maximum 4 marks

6   Aisha placed small samples of four different metals on a spotting tile.
She added drops of copper sulphate solution to each metal.

Aisha repeated the experiment with fresh samples of the four metals and solutions of different salts. She recorded some of her results in a table.

✔   shows that a reaction place   ✗   shows that no reaction took place

solutions	copper	iron	magnesium	zinc
copper sulphate	✗	✔	✔	
iron sulphate	✗	✗	✔	✔
magnesium sulphate	✗		✗	
zinc sulphate	✗	✗	✔	✗

a   The four metals have different reactivities.
(i) Use the information in the table to put the four metals in a reactivity series.

most reactive metal   ....

....

....

least reactive metal   ....
(1 mark)

(ii) Use the reactivity series to complete the table by writing ✔ or ✗ in the
three empty boxes.
(2 marks)

b Copper reacts with silver nitrate solution.
(i) Complete the word equation for the reaction:

Copper + silver nitrate → .... + ... (2 marks)

(ii) Platinum does **not** react with silver nitrate. Put the metals platinum, copper and silver in the correct order according to their reactivity.

most reactive metal ....

....

least reactive metal .... (1 mark)

c In many houses the hot water pipes are made from copper and the boiler is made from iron. Which of these metals will corrode first? Explain your answer.

.... (1 mark)

maximum 7 marks

7 A father makes a simple mobile for his young son. He uses plastic animals as shown.

a (i) The elephant weighs 0.2 N. What is the turning moment produced by the elephant about point X? Give the unit.

....(1 mark)

....(1 mark)

(ii) What is the turning moment produced by the monkey about point X?

....

....(1 mark)

(iii) What is the weight of the monkey?

.... N (1 mark)

b What is the size of the tension (force) in string A?

.... N (1 mark)

maximum 5 marks

8   Karen wants to pump up her car tyre.
Her pump has a piston with an area of 7 cm^2

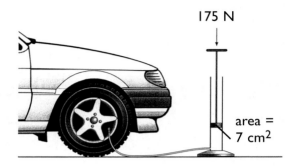

175 N

area =
7 cm^2

Karen pushes the handle down with a force of 175 N.

a   What pressure does she exert on the air in the pump?

....N/cm^2 *(1 mark)*

b   The air pressure in the tyre is 27 N/cm^2.
What pressure would be needed **in the pump** in order to pump more air
into the tyre?

....   *(1 mark)*

c   Another of Karen's car tyres exerts a pressure of 30 N/cm^2 on the road.
The area of the tyre in contact with the road is 95 cm^2.
What is the force exerted by the tyre on the road?

....N   *(1 mark)*

maximum 3 marks

9   **a**   A pupil makes a small coil of copper wire and passes an electric current
through it.
The pupil places a small magnet near the coil.

coil   N   S   magnet

The magnet is attracted towards the coil.
The pupil turns the magnet around
so that the South pole is nearest the coil.
What effect, if any, will this have?

....

....   *(1 mark)*

b The pupil uses the coil and the magnet to make a simple ammeter to measure the current through a bulb.

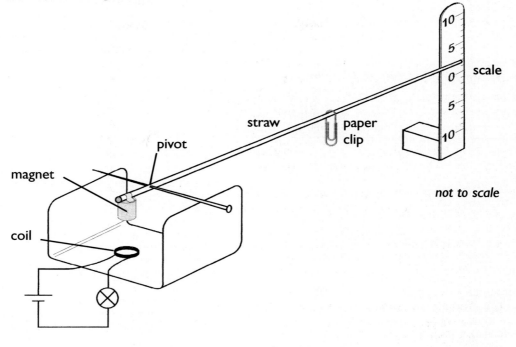

not to scale

(i) The paper clip is used to balance the weight of the magnet.
Why is the paper clip further away from the pivot than the magnet is?

....

....

(1 mark)

(ii) Explain how a current in the coil makes the straw pointer move.

....

....

(2 marks)

(iii) The pupil places a piece of soft iron in the middle of the coil.
Describe and explain how this will affect the reading on the scale when the same current flows through the coil.

....

....

(2 marks)

maximum 6 marks

total possible marks 53

total marks ☐

LEVEL 5

1 SCIENTIFIC ENQUIRY – ALL ABOUT GRAPHS (page 2)

Q1

Speed of car (miles per hour)	Driver's thinking distance (m)	Braking distance (m)	Total stopping distance (m)
20	6	6	12
30	9	14	23
40	12	24	36
50	15	38	53
60	18	55	73
70	21	75	96

Q2 Horizontal axis should show speed of car in miles per hour, be labelled and have intervals of 10 mph.

Vertical axis should be labelled correctly as Total stopping distance in metres, and have intervals of 10 or 20. The result should therefore look like this.

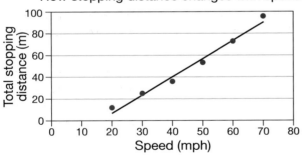

How stopping distance changes with speed

From this graph, stopping distance at 45 mph and 65 mph should be read off as 46 m and 84 m respectively, depending on exactly where the line of best fit has been drawn.

COMMENT Total stopping distance is calculated by adding the driver's thinking distance and braking distance. When plotting a graph make sure that you label your axes carefully showing the units. In this question to have labelled the axes 'Speed' and 'Total stopping distance' without adding the units of miles per hour and metres would have been incorrect.

When you draw a line on a graph remember to draw a straight line or a smooth curve taking in as many points as possible – this is the line of best fit. Don't just join up the points in a 'dot-to-dot' way.

Q3 Height, hand span and length of little finger are continuous variables.

Shoe size, eye colour, gender and hair colour are discontinuous variables.

COMMENT Remember that continuous variables can have any value within their range. Discontinuous variables have a fixed set of possible values.

2 CLASSIFICATION (page 6)

Q1

Name of invertebrate	Group it belongs to
Spider	arthropod
Slug	molluscs
Jelly fish	coelenterates
Tapeworm	flatworms
Earthworm	annelids

COMMENT Remember that 'arthropods' is a group that includes all the animals with a hard external skeleton and jointed legs: the insects, arachnids, myriapods (centipedes and millipedes) and crustaceans.

Q2 a Mammals. They have hair or fur and give birth to live young. The young feed on their mother's milk.
b Birds. They have feathers and lay hard-shelled eggs on land.
c Amphibians. They have smooth, damp skin, live on both land and water and lay their soft-shelled eggs in water.
d Fish. Fish have scales, fins and gills and live in water.
e Reptiles. Reptiles have hard, dry scales and lay their soft-shelled eggs on land.

COMMENT The differences between birds, mammals and fish are very straightforward. However, you should be careful not to confuse reptiles and amphibians. Remember that amphibians do not have scales. They have smooth, moist skin. Reptiles have dry scales. Also, amphibians live in both water and on land and always lay their eggs in water. Reptiles always lay their eggs on the land.

It is useful for you to be able to draw classification charts for the different kingdoms. Look back at the charts in this chapter. For the animal kingdom, you start off by splitting the animals into those with backbones and those without backbones. The vertebrates can be split into groups of mammals, birds, fish, amphibians and reptiles. You should try to find a way of remembering these groups and groups within other kingdoms, and eventually you can build up a chart that contains all living things.

Q3

Group	Things they have in common	Example
Algae	no roots, stems or leaves	seaweed
Mosses	simple stems and leaves, make spores	moss, sphagnum
Ferns	have roots, stems and leaves, make spores	bracken
Conifers	have roots, stems and leaves, seeds grow inside cones	Scots pine
Flowering plants	have roots, stems, leaves and flowers, seeds are made inside the ovary	rose

COMMENT Plants are classified largely on the basis of how they reproduce (using seeds or spores). Check back to the chart for the plant kingdom. It shows the seed-producing plants on one side and the spore-producers on the other. Looking at the photographs will help you to remember that they are also classified according to whether they have a body with a clearly developed stem, root and leaf system.

3 HABITAT AND ADAPTATION (page 10)

Q1 **a** Spikes instead of leaves to reduce water loss.
b Very short flowering and fruiting cycle to take advantage of rainfall when it does happen.
c Thick succulent stems to retain as much moisture as possible.

COMMENT These are the sorts of questions you can answer from a mixture of scientific knowledge and common sense. It is important to practise applying what you know to unfamiliar situations.

Q2

Characteristic	Reason
Thick winter coat	To keep warm and dry in winter
Loss of thick coat in spring and much thinner summer coat	To keep cool in summer
Carnivore able to eat range of insects and small mammals	Variety of food because what is available may change at different times of year
Not too much exposed skin even in summer	Exposed skin would lose heat in winter and water in summer
Good eyesight	Able to hunt for food at night when more prey may be about during the hot dry summer

COMMENT These are just suggestions – there could be many others. Look at your answers and decide if the characteristicss you have suggested and the reasons for them make sense! Once again, answering this question relies on applying your knowledge in a situation that is possibly unfamiliar.

4 BODY ORGANS (page 13)

Q1 The functions of the digestive system are:
breaking down food;
absorbing food into the blood stream;
carrying food from one place to another.

Q2 The main functions of the circulatory system are: transport of substances around the body; defending the body against disease.

Q3 a – 5 b – 7 c – 4 d – 3 e – 1 f – 2 g – 6

COMMENT Arteries and veins are easily confused. Arteries carry blood away from the heart. The arteries have thick walls to withstand high blood pressure. Veins return blood to the heart. Because this blood has been around the body, it is at a low pressure. The veins have valves to stop the blood from flowing backwards.

Perhaps one of the most important things is to be clear about which system an organ belongs to. This will help you to remember its function. The stomach belongs to the digestive system, so it must have something to do with digestion and not pumping blood.

5 FUNCTIONS OF PLANT ORGANS (page 17)

Q1 To make biomass from water and carbon dioxide (to carry out photosynthesis) or to allow gas exchange of carbon dioxide and oxygen between the inside of the leaf and the atmosphere.

COMMENT Leaves contain the green coloured chemical called chlorophyll. This is the important chemical that allows photosynthesis to take place. Leaves have specialised cells that perform other functions and these are described in Unit 3, Revision Session 2.

Q2 Sexual reproduction is the function of a flower. The flower makes seeds after pollination and fertilisation. The seeds grow into new plants.

COMMENT The only function of the flower is sexual reproduction. It is not the job of a flower to look pretty or to smell nice, but to bring about the successful joining of a pollen grain with an ovule.

Q3 Three functions of the root are to:
anchor the plant in the soil;
take up water;
take up minerals.

COMMENT It is important to make it clear that roots take up minerals and water – not food. Plants make biomass from water and carbon dioxide using light energy from the Sun.

Q4 The anther is the male part of the flower and it makes pollen grains. Pollen grains are the male sex cell. Pollen needs to be transferred to the stigma, either by wind or by insects. Brightly coloured petals help to attract insects. The sticky stigma holds the pollen grains. The pollen joins with the female sex cell (the ovule) and fertilises it. The fertilised ovules develop into seeds inside the ovary.

6 THE PROPERTIES OF METALS (page 20)

Q1

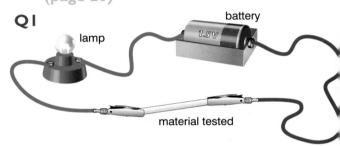

Set this apparatus up and put the material to be tested between the two crocodile clips. If the bulb lights up, the material must be a conductor.

COMMENT The only way to test whether a material conducts electricity or not is to make it part of an electrical circuit. You must have something there to show that the electricity is flowing. In this case, it is a bulb which lights up. If the bulb lights, the material conducts electricity.

Q2 METAL – good conductor of electricity, good thermal conductor, shiny, usually silvery, usually high melting point, flexible, usually strong

NON-METAL – poor conductor of electricity, poor thermal conductor, dull, different colours, usually low melting point, brittle, usually weak

COMMENT You have to be familiar with some of the properties, so have a go at writing them out. Each list has the most useful property first, so start there and learn as many as you can. When you have to learn a list like this, try writing it, then check the ones you missed. Then learn those ones and have another go at writing the whole thing.

Q3 a 1 Metal   2 Non-metal   3 Non-metal
  4 Metal   5 Metal   6 Non-metal

  b Number 2

COMMENT The best property to go for is electrical
conductivity. That sorts most of them out! But you
have to be careful of the exceptions so you
cannot rely on just one property.

Substance 2 has a high melting point, is strong and
conducts electricity. A property that enables us to
decide that it is a non-metal is its poor conduction
of thermal energy. All metals conduct thermal
energy very well. In addition, metals are not black
and they are flexible.

7 EVAPORATION AND CONDENSATION (page 23)

Q1 Liquid changing to gas.

Q2 Gas changing to liquid.

COMMENT Check the summary diagram on page 24
if you did not get the correct answer to either 1 or 2.

Q3 The three factors which affect the rate of
evaporation are:
• the temperature of the water (in washing);
• the amount of water vapour present in the air
immediately above the surface of the washing;
• the speed at which the air is moving past the
surface of the washing.

COMMENT If the air close to the washing is still,
cold and full of water vapour then the rate of
evaporation from the washing will be very slow
and the washing will take a very long time to dry.

Q4 The liquid in the paint has evaporated into the
surrounding air leaving the solid part behind.

COMMENT Even when the lid is in place correctly,
evaporation takes place from the surface of the
paint but the liquid cannot escape from the tin.

Q5 Water.

COMMENT Remember that 'condensation' on a
window is actually water that has condensed on
the cold surface.

8 ELEMENTS, COMPOUNDS AND MIXTURES (page 26)

Q1

Element	Mixture	Compound
Oxygen	Air	Water
Hydrogen		Salt
Copper		Iron oxide
Nitrogen		Brass
Tin		

COMMENT Remember that elements have one kind
of atom, compounds have two or more kinds of
atoms chemically bonded together and in a mixture
you may have any number of elements and
compounds making up the substance but with no
chemical reactions having taken place. Always
take care to use the right words. For example, don't
write 'air' if you mean 'oxygen' as air is a mixture of
a large number of elements and compounds.

Q2

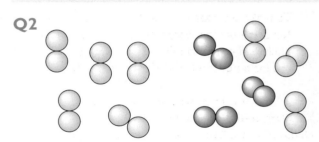

a) a pure element

b) a mixture of
   elements

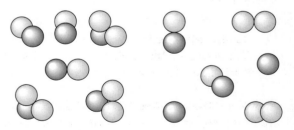

c) a mixture of
   compounds

d) a mixture of one
   compound and
   two elements

COMMENT The mixtures here have the same number
of molecules of each element or compound.
However, this is not always the case.

9 SEPARATING MIXTURES
(page 28)

Q1 a The copper sulphate dissolves (giving a blue solution) and the sand does not dissolve.

b The sand collects in the filter paper and the copper sulphate solution passes straight through.

c The copper sulphate is best obtained by evaporation.

COMMENT Remember soluble means it dissolves and insoluble means it does not.

Did you go through your checklist? If the question says soluble/insoluble then filtration is the answer. The insoluble part is trapped by the filter paper because the grains of sand are too big to pass through. Copper sulphate is a blue soluble solid, so it forms a blue solution and can pass through the filter paper.

Q2 Using distillation. Heat the sea water in a flask until it boils. The steam passes into the condenser and cools to form water. The salt is left behind in the flask.

COMMENT Water boils to form a gas and passes into the condenser. This gas condenses to form water.

Q3 Fractional distillation.

COMMENT All oils are liquids, so fractional distillation can be used to separate them.

Q4 The water evaporates into the atmosphere without being collected.

COMMENT If you want to collect the water you must condense it back to a liquid first. Evaporation is only suitable for collecting the solid from a solution, e.g. salt from sea water.

Q5

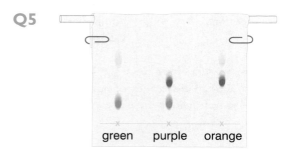

green   purple   orange

COMMENT When doing chromatography, it is important to realise that:
each type of dye will travel to a particular level;
different dyes travel to different levels.

10 VISION AND REFLECTION
(page 31)

Q1 A and D

COMMENT If you draw in the normal on each diagram you can see whether:
the angle of incidence = the angle of reflection.

The two angles are equal in A. In D, the angles are both zero. A ray of light travelling along the normal must be reflected back along the same path.

Q2

Alex can see the cat.

COMMENT Always use a ruler to draw rays of light. Do not forget to show that the light is travelling from the tree to Alex's eye, by putting arrows on the ray.

To draw the rays, first draw a line from the eye to the lower mirror. Then draw in the normal at this point. You can now draw the ray hitting the upper mirror.

Remember that:
the angle of incidence = the angle of reflection.

Now continue the ray to the top mirror and again draw the normal so that you can draw the ray of light from the tree.

Q3 a Ms Wong can see their reflection in the mirrors next to the blackboard.

b

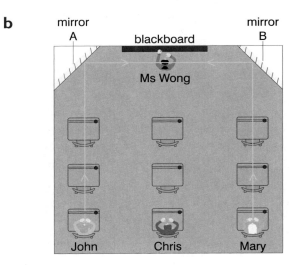

c In order to see Chris, Ms Wong needs to move one of the mirrors:

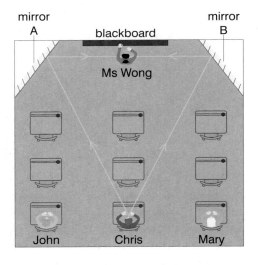

COMMENT The only way that Ms Wong can see behind her is by looking in a mirror.

Draw the ray of light from Ms Wong to the mirror, then draw in the normal at that point. Next, draw the ray of light from the pupil to the mirror, making sure that the angle of incidence = the angle of reflection.

11 SOUND (page 34)

Q1 a B

b C

c A and C

d A and B

e B

COMMENT

a The waves in B are close together; they have a shorter wavelength.

b The amplitude of the note in C is less than A and B, so C must be the quietest note.

c The waves in A and C are the same length; there are the same number of waves on the screen.

d The waves in A and B are the same height; therefore, they have the same amplitude.

e Part e has the same answer as part a. This is just checking that you understand a note with a high frequency has a high pitch.

Q2 a

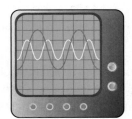

b Jim's whistle has the greater frequency.

COMMENT The wave representing Tony's whistle must be twice as tall as Jim's if it is twice as loud. The wavelength must be longer than Jim's as the pitch is lower. There will be fewer waves of Tony's whistle displayed on the screen.

12 THE MOVEMENT OF THE EARTH (page 37)

Q1

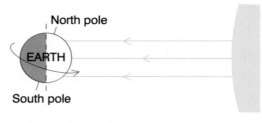

North pole

EARTH

South pole

c day

> **COMMENT** The Earth spins from west to east (the Sun rises in New York 5 hours after it has risen in Manchester).
>
> When showing which part of the Earth is in darkness, make sure you draw a vertical line, not one along the Earth's axis.
>
> The North Pole is not in the dark area because light from the Sun is reaching it. Therefore, it is in daylight.

Q2 a 365 days / 1 year

b 24 hours / 1 day

c A winter
B summer

> **COMMENT** At A the southern hemisphere is tilted away from Sun and receives less sunlight than the northern hemisphere. In winter, it has shorter days and is colder.
>
> In summer, at B, the southern hemisphere receives more sunlight, is warmer and has longer days.

13 ELECTRICAL CIRCUITS (page 40)

Q1 a) a single cell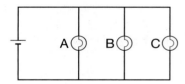

b) a lamp

c) an open switch

> **COMMENT** It is important to know the symbols for all the common electrical components and to be able to show them connected in a circuit. Remember to draw circuit diagrams as rectangles with straight lines – even though real circuits don't look like that as wires are often not at all straight.

Q2 a If bulb A breaks, bulb B will go out because this is a series circuit.

A
B

b If bulb B breaks, then bulb A will stay on and bulb C will stay on because this is a parallel circuit.

A B C

> **COMMENT** Two different symbols have been used for bulbs in the two questions. You need to know both of them and be able to use them. In these two circuits it was quite easy to see which was the series and which was the parallel – be prepared to see them drawn in ways that are less straightforward.

LEVEL 6

I SCIENTIFIC ENQUIRY – IDEAS AND EVIDENCE (page 50)

Q1 a The following would not be of any value in this survey.

How old they are
How tall they are
Their eye colour
Their hair colour

COMMENT For this survey all that they need to find out is whether each person is male or female and their shoe size.

Q1 b Asking everyone in the school would make the survey better as it would increase the chance of having enough evidence from which to draw reliable conclusions.

COMMENT For investigations using a survey, the more results you can have, the more reliable your conclusions will be. However, you must have more results for the right kind of variables. Asking one hundred people what colour their eyes are does nothing to help the reliability of a conclusion about the relationship between gender and shoe size!

Q2

Enquiry	Independent variable	Dependent variable	Control variable
Whether exercise affects pulse rates	Amount of exercise

Avoid terms like amount as they are not precise enough. Better to say length of time for which exercise is taken, number of skips, number of press-ups etc. This makes clearer exactly what you mean. | Pulse rate

Again this could be more precise. Better to say pulse rate before and after exercise – and the difference between the two. | Fitness of the people taking part

This is not a variable that can be controlled. Alternatives would be nature of exercise, rest period beforehand. |

Enquiry	Independent variable	Dependent variable	Control variable
Which paper towel is the most absorbent	Different kinds of paper towel

This is suitable | Amount of water

Again too vague – better always to say volume rather than amount. Also need to specify the condition you are observing e.g. volume of water absorbed before the towel tears or maximum volume of water absorbed by the towel. | Temperature of the water

This is not a sensible control variable. The surface area (size) of the piece of paper towel tested would be much better. |
| Where woodlice most like to live | Conditions for woodlice to choose

Be precise. Say what choices the woodlice will have. | How long it takes for the woodlice to make their choice

Far better to look at the number of woodlice who have chosen a particular condition after a set period of time. | The size of the woodlice

The size of the woodlice would be very difficult to control and would not affect the experiment. Better to make sure that there is the same amount of space with each condition and the woodlice are kept in the same conditions immediately before they are given their choice. |
| What conditions are the best for growing broad bean plants
Too vague – you would have to say: Does the amount of water affect the growth of bean plants? | Amount of water

Volume not amount! | Height of bean plants

This is suitable | The size of the plant pot

This may have an effect – but what about how often the plants are watered? e.g. if one were given 100 ml all at once and one were given 10 ml a day for each of 10 days. |

Enquiry	Independent variable	Dependent variable	Control variable
What material is best for insulating cups of hot drinks	Temperature of the drinks	How long it takes for the liquid to reach room temperature	The size and shape of the containers.
	The temperature of the drinks would need to be the same at the start of the experiment. But this is a control variable. The independent variable in this investigation needs to be the material the containers are made of.	*Or the temperature of the liquid at one minute intervals for 10 minutes.*	*This is suitable*

COMMENT Often what was wrong involved the use of **language** as well as science. It would be no good being the most brilliant scientist ever if you were not able to explain what you meant in ways that other people could understand. This is true in tests and exams as well. You must take care to use the right words so that the person reading your answers knows just what a good scientist you are.

2 VARIATION (page 52)

Q1 All of the following are possible types of variation between humans:

hair colour, eye colour, height, weight, nose shape, the accent you speak with, curly hair or straight hair, intelligence, blood group, the ability to roller-skate, the language you speak, skin colour, mouth shape, hand span, freckles and moles – and so on (there are many more).

COMMENT Any possible difference between people is acceptable here.

Q2 The missing words are shown in bold:

Children **inherit** some features from their parents. For example, **eye** colour, **hair** colour and **nose** shape are all features that are passed on from parents to their children. Each child

gets **half** their inherited information from their **mother/father** and **half** from their **father/mother**. The inherited information from the father is carried inside the **sperm** and the mother's part of the information is carried in the **egg**. These two sets of information are brought together when the sperm **joins** with the egg. This is called **fertilisation**.

COMMENT Look carefully at the text if you are not sure of the word used to complete the passage.

Q3 The table should be completed as shown below:

only the environment causes these:	inherited information causes these:	both the environment and inherited information causes these:
the accent you speak with	natural hair colour	height
the ability to roller-skate	eye colour	weight
	nose shape	intelligence
	blood group	
	naturally curly hair	

COMMENT It is important that you understand the difference between environmental and inherited causes of variation, and also that many types of variation have both environmental and inherited causes. There is an interaction between the inherited information of the person and the environment that they grow up in. The way they are brought up has an effect on the information that they inherited from their parents. Only a few features are controlled solely by the inherited information or by the effects of their environment.

If in this question we talked about 'hair colour' rather than natural hair colour, then we could talk about hair colour sometimes being environmentally controlled, such as when people dye their hair. Even natural hair colour can be influenced by the environment – many people's hair lightens when it is in the sun for a long time. So even some of the more obviously inherited features can in some circumstances be influenced by the environment.

3 CELL STRUCTURE (page 55)

Q1

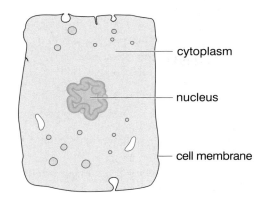

cytoplasm

nucleus

cell membrane

COMMENT A very common mistake is to label the cell membrane as the cell wall. Remember only plant cells have a cell wall – animal cells never have a cell wall.

Q2 Cell membrane, nucleus, cytoplasm.

COMMENT If you said vacuoles, you need to make it clear that plant cells always have a large central vacuole, whereas some animal cells may have a number of small, temporary vacuoles. Both can have food stores in the cell but in plant cells this will often be starch and in animal cells it will never be starch.

Q3 A: cytoplasm, B: cell membrane, C: cell wall, D: nucleus, E: starch grain, F: chloroplast, G: large central vacuole.

COMMENT Check that you have labelled the cell wall and cell membrane correctly.

Q4

Plant cells have	Animal cells have
a cell wall	no cell wall
chloroplasts	no chloroplasts
starch grains	no starch grains, but may store food as fat or glycogen
a regular box-like shape	a wide variety of shapes
large central vacuole	no large central vacuole, but may have a number of small vacuoles

COMMENT Plant cells have several things that animal cells do not have. In a test question asking about differences between cells it is better to stick to very clear differences such as the cell wall, chloroplasts and the fact that plant cells always have a large central vacuole.

4 PHOTOSYNTHESIS (page 59)

Q1 Plants produce biomass by using light energy to produce glucose from carbon dioxide and water. This is called photosynthesis.

COMMENT Plants do not get food from the soil. Plants get water and minerals from the soil which are both important in the production of biomass by photosynthesis.

Q2

Inputs	Outputs
carbon dioxide	glucose
water	oxygen
light energy	

COMMENT Carbon dioxide and water are the raw materials needed to build up the glucose molecules. The light energy may come from the Sun or artificial lighting. In photosynthesis, light energy becomes chemical energy stored in the glucose molecules. This stored energy is released by the plant in respiration. (*See Unit 3 Revision Session 4, Respiration*)

Q3 The leaf:
- contains lots of specialised cells that are packed with chloroplasts. The chloroplasts contain the green substance chlorophyll. Chlorophyll absorbs sunlight and makes the energy from the sun available for the process of photosynthesis.
- has a large surface area so that it can absorb sunlight efficiently.
- has many tiny holes called stomata that allow carbon dioxide to pass in and oxygen to pass out during the day.
- has veins that carry water into it from the roots. The part of the plant's veins that carries water is called the xylem.

Q4

a

$$\text{carbon dioxide} + \text{water} \xrightarrow{\text{light energy}} \text{glucose} + \text{oxygen}$$

b The gardener could make the plants grow faster by speeding up photosynthesis.

She could:
- increase the amount of carbon dioxide in the greenhouse;
- make sure the plants have a good water supply;
- shine lights on the tomato plants overnight, so that the plants get light 24 hours a day (this means that they will be photosynthesising all the time);
- make the lights brighter and have them come on if the day becomes too dull and cloudy.

COMMENT All of these things would make the tomato plants grow faster and make large ripe tomatoes more quickly. This is because they all make photosynthesis happen faster.

5   HEALTH AND DISEASE (page 62)

Q1 Because a 15-year-old boy is still growing – and protein is needed for growth.

Q2 A girl of 16 will lose some blood in her monthly menstrual cycle. She will need iron to make the new red blood cells that form part of the replaced blood.

COMMENT With both of these questions, you need to be able to relate your understanding of why we need to eat different kinds of food to real life examples.

Q3 Tonsilitis is a bacterial infection and so can be treated with antibiotics which kill bacteria. 'Flu is caused by a virus so antibiotics would be no use at all.

COMMENT It is a common mistake to think that antibiotics cure all diseases, they don't – they just kill bacteria.

Q4 Placenta.

COMMENT It is important to know about all the organs that make up the systems in the human body. If you are told the name of an organ you should be able to say what it does, and if you have the function of an organ described to you, you should be able to give its name.

6   WORD EQUATIONS (page 65)

Q1 calcium + water → calcium hydroxide + hydrogen

COMMENT The first part of the sentence tells you that calcium is put into water – calcium and water are the two reactants. You are then given the two products, calcium hydroxide and hydrogen. This word equation is partially complete with both calcium and calcium hydroxide already shown. Remember: reactants on the left and products on the right, with the reaction arrow pointing from left to right.

Q2 magnesium + oxygen → magnesium oxide

COMMENT The only product of this reaction is magnesium oxide. Just read the question. Do not go looking for more detail than is actually required.

Q3 magnesium + hydrochloric acid → magnesium chloride + hydrogen

COMMENT Make sure that the reactants – magnesium and hydrochloric acid – are written on the left, with products written on the right.

Q4 carbon dioxide + water → glucose + oxygen

COMMENT You should be familiar with the process of photosynthesis. If you are not sure, then refer to Revision Session 4 and check your understanding before you look at the equation again. Read the equation carefully to make sure you understand the order of events. Identify what reacts with what (reactants) to form the products. Do not forget the arrow to show the direction of the reaction, and the + signs between both of the reactants and both of the products.

7 PARTICLES (page 68)

Q1

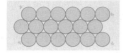 solid

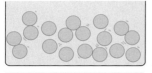 liquid

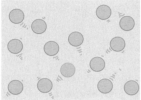 gas

a In a solid, the particles:
  • are close together;
  • are in a regular pattern;
  • vibrate about fixed points.

b In a liquid, the particles:
  • are further apart than in solids;
  • are not in any pattern;
  • move about randomly.

c In a gas, the particles:
  • are far apart;
  • are not in any pattern;
  • move about rapidly and randomly.

COMMENT A good way to learn the particle model is to be able to draw the diagrams and remember there are three things to be mentioned with each diagram:

1 how close the particles are;

2 the pattern of the particles;

3 the type of movement.

The particles become more energetic and more irregular at each stage from solid to liquid to gas.

Q2 a Melting
  Particles in a solid gain enough energy to vibrate sufficiently violently to break out of the regular pattern. As the pattern breaks down, the substance melts and becomes a liquid. The particles in a liquid move in a random way.

b Expansion
  When a solid gains more energy, the particles vibrate more (further and faster) from their central position. This causes particles to move slightly away from each other and the size of the solid increases.

c Condensation
  When particles of a gas are cooled, they slow down and come closer together until eventually enough particles come together to become a liquid.

COMMENT Look carefully at the notes on pages 68 and 69 if you find the question difficult to answer. Firstly identify the sort of change that is occurring, e.g. is it a change of state? Then consider whether the particles are gaining or losing energy before you attempt to describe the arrangement and movement of the particles.

Q3 Metamorphic rocks are formed when existing rocks are changed by the heat and pressure in the earth.

COMMENT Remember that igneous rock comes from inside the earth, so it is very hot and molten before cooling and solidifying. Sedimentary rock is made from sediment and metamorphic is the one that changes due to heat and pressure in the earth.

8 CHEMICAL REACTIONS (page 71)

Q1 a pH 7
   b pH 3
   c pH 5
   d pH 11

COMMENT Make sure that you know what the pH of various everyday substances is likely to be. You do not have to know exactly but you should know which things are generally acids and which are generally alkalis.

Q2

Physical changes	Chemical changes
a melting ice	b burning a fuel
d condensation forming on a window	c magnesium and acid reacting together

COMMENT Physical changes are quite easily reversed, and they never cause a new chemical compound to form. The process of ice melting is easily reversed (by putting it in a freezer) and the water remains water whether it is solid or liquid. Condensation is similar. The water droplets formed on a window by cooling water vapour can be changed back to water vapour by warming them.

Burning a fuel is a chemical change. It uses up the fuel and you cannot get any oil or coal back after it has been burnt. It also releases a lot of energy and forms new substances, e.g. the ash formed by burning coal is a new substance. Magnesium and acid reacting is a chemical change because it gives off hydrogen, a new substance.

Q3 Carbon dioxide

9 OXIDATION REACTIONS (page 74)

Q1 Magnesium + oxygen → magnesium oxide

Q2 Hydrogen and carbon. H and C

Q3 Carbon dioxide and water.

COMMENT

1 Word equations are just a shorthand way of describing a chemical reaction. Always make sure that any elements that appear on the left-hand side are accounted for on the right-hand side.

2 Make sure that you know the symbols for the elements that you learn about. Some, like hydrogen and carbon, are easy as they are just the initial letters of the name. Others are more difficult, like sodium which is Na.

3 Remember, respiration is not breathing. It is a chemical reaction that goes on in every cell in every animal and every plant.

10 FORCES AND MOTION (page 76)

Acceleration is when the forward arrow is bigger than the backward one.

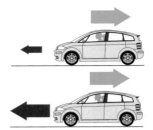

Slowing down is when the backward arrow is bigger than the forward one.

Steady speed is when the two arrows are the same size.

COMMENT Remember that arrows showing forces show both the direction and the magnitude of the force. The magnitude of the force is shown by the size of the arrow.

Q2

Speed in metres per second (m/s)	Distance in metres (m)	Time in seconds (s)
2 m/s	100	50
25 m/s	500	20
15	150	**10 s**
30	**9000 m**	300

COMMENT Practise rearranging equations so that you can calculate any particular quantity. Always remember to give the units for the result of the calculation.

11 REFRACTION (page 78)

Q1

A | normal
air
B
perspex

C Refraction

COMMENT Make sure that you use a ruler and pencil. Remember to draw the normals and arrows on the rays of light.

When light travels from air to glass, it bends towards the normal. When it leaves the glass and enters the air again, it bends away from the normal.

For a ray of light to pass through the block without bending, it does not matter where it enters the block as long as it is at right angles to the block, i.e. along the normal.

Q2

Yes, Anna can see the fish.

COMMENT The ray of light travelling from the fish to Anna's eye passes from water into air. When it reaches the boundary between the two types of medium, the ray is refracted away from the normal, so the fish appears to be in a different place than its actual position.

12 ENERGY RESOURCES (page 81)

Q1

Energy resource	Renewable	Non-renewable	From the Sun
coal		✓	✓
oil		✓	✓
gas		✓	✓
wave	✓		✓
tidal	✓		
hydroelectric	✓		✓
biomass	✓		✓
nuclear		✓	
solar	✓		✓
wind	✓		✓

COMMENT You must be clear about which energy resources are renewable and which are non-renewable. Renewable energy resources are always being replaced. Non-renewable resources will eventually run out. Geothermal energy is not included in the table – it is not renewable, but there is so much of it that it will take a very long time to be used up.

Most energy resources come originally from the Sun. Nuclear energy, geothermal energy and tidal energy do not.

Q2 The weather in the UK is variable and unpredictable. We do not get sufficient sun or wind for us to be able to rely on them as our only energy resource.

COMMENT The energy supply depends on the weather. On a sunny and windy day there will be a large supply of energy, but on a still night there will be little wind or solar energy. If this type of energy was to be used to produce electricity, an alternative would be needed for when there was little sun or wind.

Q3 a Fossil fuels are burnt in a furnace. This heat is used to boil water, to produce steam. The steam turns a turbine. The turbine turns a generator, which produces electricity.

b Wind is used to turn a turbine in a windmill, which turns a generator to produce electricity.

COMMENT There are four main parts concerned with the production of electricity in a power station where the fuel is burnt (see the flow chart on page 82).

To generate electricity, kinetic energy (movement) is needed to turn a generator. This energy can come directly from wind, wave motion, falling water (hydroelectric) and tides. The energy can also be produced by burning fuels (fossil fuels or biomass), or producing heat (nuclear fuel and geothermal). Thermal energy is used to produce steam, which makes turbines move. These produce kinetic energy (movement), which can then be used to turn the generators.

13 THE SOLAR SYSTEM (page 84)

Q1 a A star is a massive 'ball of fire' which may have planets in orbit around it.

b A planet is a large object that orbits around a star.

c A moon is an object which orbits around a planet.

COMMENT When you give these definitions, you should not refer to specific stars, planets and moons except to use them as examples.

Q2 a & b

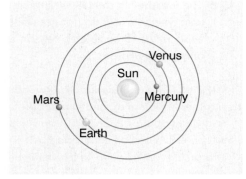

c No. Light from the Sun is much brighter than the light reflected from Mercury.

d Yes. Mars will be seen at night because it reflects the Sun's light.

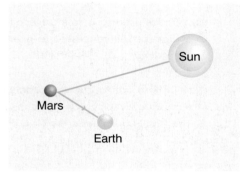

COMMENT Remember your funny sentence. Mercury is the closest planet to the Sun, next comes Venus and then Earth.

Be careful not to assume that the Sun is in the way. It may not be, because the orbits of planets in the solar system are not all in the same plane.

Remember that planets are not luminous but reflect light from the Sun.

Q3 blue star, white star, Sun, red star, Earth

COMMENT Even on a very hot day the Earth's temperature does not get anywhere near that of a cool red star.

LEVEL 7

I SCIENTIFIC ENQUIRY – EVALUATING EVIDENCE (page 93)

Q1

a This question does not have one right answer. You can say that you think that moving the hedgehogs to the mainland or killing them is the best thing to do.

b BUT your answer to this part must explain what you put in part a. Remember to explain carefully why you came to your decision.
A reason for moving the hedgehogs to the mainland could be that you believe in animal rights and that they should be allowed to survive.
A reason for killing the hedgehogs on the island could be that you believe that this is the most humane thing to do. If the hedgehogs were moved to a new environment they may have difficulty competing for food with the established animals.

c In order to evaluate the success of removing the hedgehogs, you will need to establish a control experiment (where hedgehogs are not removed). You could do this by designating two plots on the breeding site. One would be fenced to exclude hedgehogs, the other would be unfenced. For each plot you would need to collect data on the number of nests that had been established and the number of eggs that were successfully hatched.
An actual experiment conducted like this found that birds nesting in the fenced plot had two and a half times the breeding success.

COMMENT As often is the case with scientific enquiry questions, this is testing how well you can apply what you know to situations that you have probably never thought about before. Don't ever panic if you see a question about an unfamiliar situation. Just read carefully to find the information that the question actually gives you and use the knowledge that you have about the scientific ways of doing things.

2 FOOD WEBS (page 95)

Q1 a The chain must start with a plant or part of a plant. Each organism must be linked by an arrow and the arrow should point to the animal that is doing the eating.

b A food chain shows some of the feeding relationships in a habitat. It also shows in which direction food and energy pass in this particular feeding relationship.

COMMENT You may be tempted to just join the organisms in your food chain with straight lines without any arrows. This is incomplete because it does not show in which direction food and energy are passing. The food chain must have arrows with clear arrowheads pointing towards the organism that is doing the eating. For example:

grass → snowshoe hare → lynx

Q2 a Any one of the following producers: grass, clover, dandelion.

b Any one of the following consumers: field vole, field mouse, fox, barn owl.

c Any one of the following herbivores: field mouse, field vole, rabbit.

d The dandelions would increase in number.

e The fox population would decrease because they would have less food.

f The rabbits may increase in number because there is more food for them as a result of the death of the field mice. In other words there is less competition for food.
or
The number of rabbits will go down because there is now less food for the secondary consumers (foxes and barn owls). As a result, the secondary consumers will have to eat more rabbits.
or
The number of rabbits will stay more or less the same as a result of the two opposite effects described above.

g The energy comes from the Sun in the first place.

COMMENT
a Remember that a producer is a plant that makes its own biomass by photosynthesis.
b Remember a consumer is an organism that eats something else and that cannot make its own food.
c A herbivore only eats plants or plant material. The second organism in a food chain is always a herbivore.
f The different possible effects on the rabbit show that the feeding relationships in a particular habitat are very complicated. Remember to describe an effect and support it with clear reasons.

Q3 The pyramid should look like this:

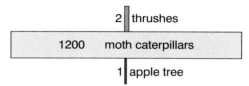

COMMENT This producer (an apple tree) is very large and has a large mass. One apple tree can feed many moth caterpillars, but these only provide food for a few thrushes.

Q4 The pyramid should look like this:

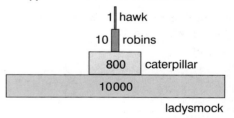

COMMENT This is a more common pyramid of numbers, where the number of the organisms at each successive level gets smaller.

3 SPECIALISED CELLS (page 99)

Q1 There are many different types of cell because each cell type has a different job to do.

Q2 A enzymes
B nucleus
C mitochondria
D tail
• the tail allows the sperm to swim from the vagina to the Fallopian tube;

- the nucleus contains half the genetic information that joins with the ovum's half of the genetic information to form a full nucleus with a whole set of genetic information;
- enzymes on the head of the sperm dissolve the ovum membrane;
- mitochondria provide energy for swimming.

COMMENT *Check the diagram on page 100 if you are not sure about the parts of this specialised cell.*

Q3

Cell	Adaptations
root hair cell	no waxy cuticle layer
	long hair-like projections from the body of the cell
palisade cell	many chloroplasts
	chloroplasts near to the upper surface of the leaf

COMMENT *Make sure you are clear which sort of cell you are considering. If you are given a diagram of a cell, look at it carefully. Its shape and structure will give you clues about its function and how its structure best enables it to perform that function.*

4 RESPIRATION (page 103)

Q1 Respiration is the release of energy from food (getting energy from food).

COMMENT *Respiration is not breathing – it is getting energy from food. Some people call breathing 'external respiration'. It is less confusing if we call breathing 'breathing' and just use the word respiration to mean releasing energy from food.*

Q2 Animals need energy to **move**, for **growth**, and for **reproduction**. Some animals use energy to keep their body at a constant **temperature**. Plants need energy for **growth**, **reproduction** and for taking up some **minerals** from the soil.

COMMENT *Plants also need energy for movement, although some plant movement is a kind of fast growth. Animals and plants do not need energy for respiration. Respiration is the way that living things get their energy.*

Q3 Aerobic respiration:

$$\text{glucose} + \text{oxygen} \xrightarrow{\text{energy is released}} \text{carbon dioxide} + \text{water}$$

COMMENT *Remember that aerobic respiration always uses oxygen and makes carbon dioxide and water as waste products.*

5 HUMAN IMPACT ON THE ENVIRONMENT (page 106)

Q1

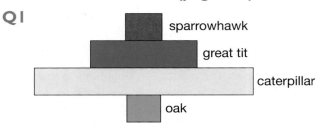

COMMENT *This is not necessarily to scale, but the point is that one oak tree will provide food for many caterpillars, a smaller number of great tits and an even smaller number of sparrowhawks.*

Q2 The amount of pesticide absorbed by the tree would not have been enough to harm it, but it would have been eaten by the caterpillars. The caterpillars again would not have had enough pesticide to cause them any harm but it would have remained in their bodies to be eaten by the tits. The same thing would have happened with each tit absorbing some pesticide every time it ate a caterpillar. When the tits were eaten by the sparrowhawks the amount of pesticide remaining in the body of each small bird they ate would eventually add up to a fatal dose for a sparrowhawk.

COMMENT *It is always important to remember that anything that affects one plant or animal in a food chain or web will always have some effect on the other organisms that live in that habitat.*

6 SYMBOLS AND FORMULAE
(page 108)

Q1

Elements	Compounds
Na	NaCl
O_2	$Ca(OH)_2$
Al	Al_2O_3
N_2	H_2O
Ne	H_2SO_4
	HCl

COMMENT In an element, all the atoms are identical. NaCl, $Ca(OH)_2$, Al_2O_3, H_2O, H_2SO_4 and HCl are compounds because they contain different atoms joined together.

Na, Al and Ne are just symbols. A symbol only represents one atom. A formula contains more than one atom. It does not matter whether they are the same or not. O_2, NaCl, $Ca(OH)_2$, Al_2O_3, H_2O, N_2, H_2SO_4 and HCl all have more than one atom in them.

In O_2, there are 2 oxygen atoms (the same type) so it is a formula for an element. In NaCl, there is a sodium atom and a chlorine atom (different types) so it is a formula for a compound.

Q2 a H_2O
b H_2SO_4

COMMENT
a To show two hydrogen atoms in the molecule, write a small 2 after the H. To represent the oxygen atom, just write O.
b Write a small 2 after the hydrogen to show that there are two hydrogen atoms. To represent one sulphur atom, just write S. A 4 after the O shows that there are four oxygen atoms.

c Na_2CO_3
d $Ca(OH)_2$
e C_2H_6

COMMENT
d This example has a hydroxide group, which we write as OH. Because there are two hydroxide groups, put brackets around the OH and write the number 2 after the brackets $(OH)_2$. Calcium is a metal, so write Ca before $(OH)_2$.

Q3 a 1 sulphur atom and 2 oxygen atoms;
b 2 iron atoms and 3 oxygen atoms;
c 1 carbon atom and 4 hydrogen atoms;
d 1 zinc atom, 2 nitrogen atoms and 6 oxygen atoms;
e 2 nitrogen atoms, 8 hydrogen atoms, 1 sulphur atom and 4 oxygen atoms.

COMMENT
a The number that tells you how many atoms there are in the compound is written after the atom, so SO_2 means 2 oxygen atoms. If no number is given then there is one atom present, so in this formula there is 1 sulphur atom.

b In this example, there is a 2 after the Fe and a 3 after the O. This means that there are 2 iron atoms in the compound for every 3 oxygen atoms.

d When a bracket is used, everything in the bracket is multiplied by the number after it. For $Zn(NO_3)_2$, there are two groups of NO_3, so for every zinc atom there are two nitrogen atoms and six oxygen atoms.

e This is similar to part d except that the bracket is around the first group of atoms. $(NH_4)_2SO_4$ can be written out as $NH_4 + NH_4 + SO_4$. This gives 2 nitrogen atoms and 8 hydrogen atoms (from the two NH_4 groups) for every 1 sulphur atom and 4 oxygen atoms.

7 WEATHERING (page 112)

Q1 a Rocks can be weathered by changes in temperature causing expansion and contraction of the rock – the forces are very strong and the rock cracks and breaks apart.

b Water can seep into the cracks in the rocks. When it freezes to form ice, it expands. The force of expansion is so great it can widen the crack in the rock. If this keeps happening, part of the rock will break away.

COMMENT Water is unusual because when it freezes it expands. If water seeps into cracks in a rock and the temperature drops below its freezing point, the water will form ice. As it does this, it expands, causing the crack to widen. The force can be large enough to cause the rock to split completely.

Q2 Acidic rainwater attacks limestone because the rock is mainly calcium carbonate. Great amounts of fossil fuels are burned in cities for heating buildings and for transport. Sulphur dioxide, formed from the impurities, makes the rain much more acidic and more reactive. In the country, this is less of a problem because there is less pollution.

COMMENT Acids are quite reactive substances and the stronger the acid, the more reactive it is. Carbon dioxide only forms a very weak acid in water, so there is very little reaction. Sulphur dioxide is an impurity from burning fossil fuels – it pollutes the atmosphere and forms a much stronger acid. It is also present in much greater amounts in a city, so the damage to limestone buildings is greater. In many cities this is a major problem, attacking the stonework of old buildings such as cathedrals.

8 REACTIVITY SERIES (page 115)

Q1 sodium and magnesium

COMMENT These are the two metals either side of calcium in the reactivity series.

Q2 zinc and tin

COMMENT These are the two metals either side of iron in the reactivity series.

Q3 silver and gold

COMMENT These two metals are so unreactive that they have not reacted with other elements in the environment and are therefore found almost pure in the ground.

Q4 a   yes   copper
b   no
c   no
d   yes   silver
e   yes   iron

COMMENT The way to make the correct predictions is to pick out the metal which is higher in the reactivity series. A more reactive metal can displace a less reactive metal from a compound or solution of a compound. The metal that is lower in the reactivity series is the one that can be displaced, so for a displacement reaction to take place, it must be in solution to start with. If magnesium is added then all the metals below it (aluminium, zinc, iron, lead, copper, silver and gold) can be displaced from their compounds.

9 ENVIRONMENTAL CHEMISTRY (page 118)

Q1 a Sulphur dioxide

b Carbon dioxide

COMMENT There is often a lot of confusion about this one – make quite sure you know which gas is responsible for what and avoid general terms like 'pollution' without explaining exactly what you mean.

Q1 Any three of these:
a The polar ice caps may melt causing sea levels to rise.
b Regions that have had temperate climates may become very hot and so the amount of desert will become greater.
c There may be more hurricanes, floods and tidal waves.
d Habitats may change causing some species of animals and plants to die out.

COMMENT Make sure you understand what is meant by global warming and what causes it. Do not get mixed up with other phenomena such as holes in the ozone layer.

10 THE COLOUR OF OBJECTS (page 120)

Q1 a Red paper with no crosses on it.

b Magenta paper with red crosses.

COMMENT
a Both the white paper and the red crosses will reflect the red light. It will all look red, so the crosses will not be seen.
b The white paper will reflect the magenta light. The crosses will reflect the red light from the magenta and absorb the blue light, so they will look red.

Q2

	White light	Blue light	Yellow light	Red light
Red hat	red	black	red	red
Green jacket	green	black	green	black
White scarf	white	blue	yellow	red
Magenta trousers	magenta	blue	black	red

COMMENT When white light shines onto an object, the object reflects all its colours, so the colour that the object appears is its actual colour. A white object will reflect the colour of the light shining on it and so appear to be the colour of the light.

A red object will only reflect red light. If no red light shines on it, it will appear black, because no light is reflected. For the same reason, blue objects will only reflect blue light.

Magenta reflects red and blue light. If neither red or blue light shines on the trousers, they appear black.

11 MOMENTS AND TURNING FORCES (page 122)

Q1 a In the centre.
b Because the weight on each side of the pivot will be the same so the ladder will be in equilibrium.

Q2 Weight A turning force = 6 N x 5 cm = 30 N cm

Weight B turning force = 3 N x 14 cm = 42 N cm

To create equilibrium, the turning force from weight A will have to be increased to 42 N cm. As weight A is 6 newtons:
Turning force 42 N cm = 6 N x 7 cm
So weight A will have to be moved 2 cm further away from the pivot.

COMMENT Questions on moments often seem quite hard but always remember that the three things you need to consider are: the size of the force, the distance from the pivot and the direction in which the force is acting. If you think about whatever diagram or description you are given in those terms then you will always be able to answer the question! If you have only been given a description then draw a sketch so that you can see how the forces are acting.

12 PRESSURE (page 124)

Q1 $\text{pressure} = \dfrac{\text{force}}{\text{area}} = \dfrac{300 \text{ N}}{6 \text{ m}^2} = 50 \text{ N/m}^2 \text{ (or Pa)}$

COMMENT Remember that the weight of an object is its force due to gravity.

Always write down the equation you are using and show all your working – even if you end up with the wrong answer you will get some marks if your working is correct.

Do not forget to give the units – you will lose marks if you miss them out.

Q2 Wide tyres will stop the tractor from sinking into the mud. The area in contact with the ground is large, so the pressure on the ground is lower than if it had thin tyres.

COMMENT Always comment on what effect the area has on the pressure.

Q3 a The largest pressure is exerted when the surface area in contact with the sand is smallest (1 m x 2 m = 2 m²):

$\text{pressure} = \dfrac{\text{force}}{\text{area}} = \dfrac{30 \text{ N}}{2 \text{ m}^2} = 15 \text{ Pa}$

b The smallest pressure is exerted when the surface area in contact with the sand is largest (2 m x 3 m = 6 m²):

$\text{pressure} = \dfrac{\text{force}}{\text{area}} = \dfrac{30 \text{ N}}{6 \text{ m}^2} = 5 \text{ Pa}$

c a

COMMENT Remember to show your working and give units.

When the box is placed on its smallest side, the pressure will be greatest. The box will sink further into the sand when the pressure is 15 Pa, as in part a.

Q4 a 600 N

b $\text{pressure} = \dfrac{\text{force}}{\text{area}} = \dfrac{600}{3000} = 0.2 \text{ N/cm}^2$

c Chris' feet have a much smaller area in contact with the snow than when he is on the snowboard.

COMMENT

a This is the force due to the weight of Chris and his snowboard.

b The area is given in cm² so make sure that the pressure is in N/cm².

c The weight of Chris and his snowboard does not change, but the pressure exerted by his feet is six times the pressure of when he is on the snowboard. Therefore, the area of the snowboard must be six times bigger than the combined area of Chris' feet. The area of his feet is one sixth of 3000 cm² (500 cm² total or 250 cm² each).

13 ELECTROMAGNETS (page 127)

Q1 Place a (soft) iron core inside the coil.
Add more turns to the coil.
Increase the current flowing through the coil.

Q2 An electric current flows through the coil.
The coil becomes magnetised.
The iron rocker is attracted to the coil.
The switch contacts are closed.
A current flows in the motor circuit.

COMMENT A relay is used in a car. The starter motor needs a very large current that passes through short thick wires. The relay is used so that the key on the dashboard can switch on a circuit with a small current, which in turn completes the circuit allowing the large current to flow through the starter motor.

You may be asked questions on electromagnetic devices that you have never seen before. Look at the coil to see what is attracted to it when it is magnetised. From there you should be able to work out what happens next, and the rest of the sequence of events.

TEST ANSWERS

Question	Answer	Mark	Examiner's comments
1a	A: insects B: amphibians C: molluscs D: reptiles	1 1 1 1	Check the observable features of each animal before using only one of the six words in the list to name the group to which each animal belongs.
b	A C	2	Your answers can be in any order but you must make sure that you use the letters of the animals. Invertebrates are animals without a backbone.
2a	Initial temperature of water Exclusion of drafts Volume or mass of water Surface area of water	1 for each of two correct answers	You could say the shape or size of the container and that would also get you the mark – but if you think about the scientific reason for that, it is to do with the surface area of the water.
b	They have not collected (or recorded) data about temperature	1	The question asks if their results were sufficient to test their prediction – as their prediction was about the relationship between temperature and evaporation their results do not relate to their prediction.
c	The line should be straight	1	A line of best fit should be the best straight line or smooth curve taking in as many points as possible – not just joining up the dots as has been done here.
d	6 points correctly plotted	1	Correctly plotted means accurate to half a square – this needs a sharp pencil and careful plotting!
e	A straight line of best fit taking in as many of the points as possible	1	Don't make the same mistake as is shown in the question.
f	Tick in the box for room 2 and a correct explanation such as the volume goes down more quickly or the points are lower for room 2	1	
3a	minerals or mineral salts	1	You will also get the mark if you refer to substances such as nitrate, phosphate or something general such as 'salt'. However, the names of specific elements such as nitrogen and potassium will not get the mark.
b	Any **one** from • it covers a wide area • they can reach deeper • they have a large surface area	1	You will also get the mark if you refer to the roots reaching a long way from the plant or that they would have more root hairs.
c	Any **one** from • photosynthesis cannot take place • photosynthesis takes place in the leaves	1	Having lost its leaves the sites of photosynthesis are no longer present and biomass is not being produced.
d	Any **two** from • it is camouflaged • it is shaped like a twig • it is the same colour **or** pattern as a twig • the birds **or** predators do not see it **or** eat it	2	You will also get the mark if you refer to the fact that the caterpillar looks like a twig or branch or a bit of tree and is therefore difficult to see as it blends in with the background. This helps it survive because it does not get eaten.
4a(i)	Any **one** from • gold • iron • magnesium	1	Read the text in the box carefully before answering any of the questions. Look for the clues in the text – conduction of electricity is a characteristic of all metals.

a(ii)	Any **one** from • sulphur • phosphorus	I	With one exception, carbon, non-metals do not conduct electricity.
a(iii)	iron	I	You will be expected to know that iron rusts.
a(iv)	iron sulphide	I	Compounds are produced when two or more substances react with each other to produce a new substance.
b	magnesium sulphide	I	The clue is in the text. Iron and sulphur react to form iron sulphide. So this is the product of the reaction between magnesium and sulphur. You will not get the mark if you suggest the formation of either magnesium sulphite or magnesium sulphate.
5a	solution insoluble solvent	3	Only use the words provided in the list. Answers must be in the correct order.
b	Any **one** from • filter it / filtration • pour off the liquid	I	
c	it evaporated	I	Even room temperature is high enough for some particles to have enough energy to evaporate. Overnight the solvent evaporated leaving the brown solid behind in the dish. You will also get the mark if you describe that the water had become a gas or vapour.
d	condensing	I	Condensation takes place when a gas cools and turns to liquid. If you tick more than one box you will not get the mark.
6a(i)	The point at (60,33) circled.	I	The anomalous result is the one that does not appear to fit with the pattern in the data. This point looks lower than it ought and does not fit with the gentle curve that could be drawn to join all of the points plotted on the graph.
a(ii)	A smooth curve touching all points except the anomalous point at 60°C.	I	The curve must be near or touch all points except the anomalous point. To get the mark this must be a single line not a series of dot-to-dot lines and the line must not be so thick that the points are not visible.
a(iii)	38	I	Read the point where the line you have drawn on the graph crosses the vertical 60°C line. You will get the mark for any value of mass between 37 g and 39 g.
b	Any **one** from: • they measured mass or temperature inaccurately • they failed to make sure the solution was saturated • the solution had cooled	I	To get this mark you must be specific and identify a mistake in the experimental procedure. Stating that Sarah had not given enough time for the dissolving or did not stir the solution properly will also get the mark. Answers referring to carelessness and writing things down inaccurately will not be specific enough to get the mark.
7a	off off off off on on on on on on off off	I I I	The whole row must be correct in each case to get the mark.
b	either close S4 and S5 OR leave S3 ONLY open	I	It is not enough to say leave S3 open without saying that it is the only one to be left open as S4 and S5 must both be closed.
8a	the balloon vibrates	I	John's voice vibrates the air in front of his mouth and these vibrations pass through the air and cause the balloon to vibrate.

b	it vibrates more strongly	I	You would also get the mark if you said the vibrations are bigger or that the balloon moves/vibrates more.
c	60-120 decibels	I	The bursting balloon will make a sound louder than normal speech but not as loud as a road drill. Only tick one box. You will lose the mark if you put a tick in more than one box.
d(i)	burst ear drum	I	You could also get the mark for describing that the loud sounds could make you deaf or cause tinnitus, which is a continual ringing in the ear.
d(ii)	Any **one** from • wear ear defenders • use ear plugs	I	Ears can be protected in very noisy places by stopping the sound from entering the ear.
9a	horizontal arrow pointing to the left	I	As the Moon is casting a shadow on the surface of the Earth, the Sun must be to the left of the Moon. The arrow may be drawn anywhere on the diagram.
b	towards the South	I	Great Britain is in the Northern Hemisphere of the Earth. Even in mid-summer you look South when looking towards the Sun. Make sure that you do not tick more than one box. You will not get the mark if you do.
c	Any **one** from • the part of the shadow which passes over Padstow is narrower • the part of the shadow which passes over Falmouth is wider or bigger	I	The shadow of the Moon moves across the surface of the Earth at a constant speed. However, it is disc-shaped being narrower at the ends than it is in the middle.
d	Any **one** from • the Moon moves around the Earth • the Earth spins on its axis	I	You will also get the mark if you refer to the Earth turning, rotating or going around. Make sure that you do not refer to the Earth moving around the Sun or to the Sun itself moving.

LEVEL 6

Question	Answer		Mark	Examiner's comments
1a	it helps to hide it from its prey it helps to hide it from predators		2	Make sure that you make two statements, one for each of the two marks. Your answers may be in any order.
b	inherit genes nuclei		3	Only use words from the list that is given in the question.
2a	A: membrane B: nucleus C: cytoplasm		3	The diagram shows a typical animal cell. You will be expected to know the names of these parts of the cell.
b	Any **two** from • cell wall • chloroplasts • large vacuole		2	These are the three parts which plant cells have but animal cells do not.
c(i)	part	letter of part	4	Look at the diagram carefully to check which part of the cell is indicated by the arrow and labelled with which letter.
	cell wall	D		
	cytoplasm	F		
	nucleus	A		
	vacuole	C		

c(ii)	Any **two** from • A • E • F	2	All cells have a nucleus, a cell membrane and cytoplasm. Plant cells also have chloroplasts, a cell wall and vacuoles.
3a	glucose	1	Glucose is the product of photosynthesis. You would also get the mark for describing it as sugar or a carbohydrate.
b(i)	to absorb enough or more light	1	Sunlight is essential for photosynthesis. In order to capture enough for the process, plants in shady places have large leaves.
b(ii)	chloroplasts	1	The green pigment chlorophyll is contained within the chloroplasts.
4a(i)	549.8 g	1	The bottle is sealed – nothing can get either in or out. After one week the mass of the bottle and its contents will not have changed. The balance will show the same reading as it did the week before.
a(ii)	mass does not change in a reaction	1	The total mass of the substances in the bottle will remain constant even though a chemical reaction has taken place. Mass is conserved during chemical reactions.
b(i)	iron + oxygen → iron (III) oxide	1	The whole word equation is required for the mark. You must refer to oxygen and not air in the word equation because that is the element that takes part in the reaction. It is acceptable to write 'iron oxide' rather than the full name as given in the word equation.
b(ii)	oxidation	1	This is the name of the reaction for the combination with oxygen.
5a(i)	they increase	1	You will also get the mark if you describe the object as expanding or getting bigger.
a(ii)	they will decrease	1	The concrete sections of the road expand in both directions making the gaps get smaller.
a(iii)	they might bend or crack or break up	1	The ends of the road sections would not have the space to allow for the expansion and push against each other causing damage.
b	so that it can flow when the gaps get smaller	1	You will also get the mark if you refer to the tar getting squeezed or squashed allowing the concrete to expand so that it does not get damaged.
6a	No **and** Any **one** from: • sulphuric acid did not cure scurvy • not all of the sailors recovered • only two pairs recovered • only those with fruit-related additions recovered • some with the acid failed to recover • a week is not long enough to show the effect	1	You need **both** the answer and the explanation to get the mark. If both boxes are ticked then you will not get the mark even if your explanation is correct. Any piece of evidence available from the table, which is not consistent with (is opposite to) the prediction made by James Lind will support the answer.
b(i)	Any **one** from: • addition to their diet • food **or** drink supplements • type of acid	1	An independent variable is one which is changed during the experiment. You will not get the mark if you make vague reference to type of food or drink.

b(ii)	Any **one** from: • whether they recovered • return to health • recovery from scurvy • effect after one week	I	A dependent variable is one which changes as a result of the changes made to the independent variables during the experimental procedure.
c	Any **one** from: • there must be a different substance • something in the fruits cures scurvy	I	A prediction is a statement that can be tested using an experiment. The evidence in the question showed that it was not the acid which cured scurvy. It must have been something else in the fruit which cured this disease.
d	Any **one** from: • effects due to diet may take more than a week to reveal themselves • the body takes time to adjust to the diet • time is needed for the results to reveal themselves • the effects do not take place before the week • the longer the time the more reliable the results	I	In order to make secure and valid conclusions it is important to be able to ensure that the changes in diet are actually those bringing about the observed or measured effects. In this case you have to be sure which changes to diet are providing the cure for scurvy.
7a	Q	I	For the ray of light to pass through a glass block without being refracted it must have entered and left the block at an angle of 90°.
b	P	I	Only the mirror can turn the ray of light through 90°.
c	S	I	The ray of light has been refracted towards the normal as it enters the glass prism and away from the normal as it leaves the glass prism.
d	R	I	The ray of light has been refracted towards the normal as it enters the glass block and is refracted by the same amount in the other direction (away from the normal) as it leaves the block. The ray leaving the block is therefore parallel to the ray entering the block.
8a	A	I	If the question asks for a letter from a labelled diagram you must give the letter. The answer 'upwards' would not get you the mark in this question.
b	He will remain stationary OR he will continue moving at a steady speed. There is no net force or the pairs of forces are equal.	I I	It is easy to remember that objects experiencing balanced forces remain stationary but don't forget that if the objects are moving they carry on moving in the same direction at the same speed.
c		I	In this case the arrow only had to show the direction of the force – but remember that sometimes arrows can be used to show forces of different sizes by having arrows of different sizes

Question	Answer	Mark	Examiner's comments
9a	A letter E to show that the Earth has travelled through 90° of its orbit 	1	Three months is $\frac{1}{4}$ of a year so you must show that the Earth has moved $\frac{1}{4}$ of the way around its orbit. You must make sure that you mark the letter E on the Earth's orbit.
b(i)	A letter M to show that Mars has travelled through less than 90° of its orbit	1	You only have to show the approximate position of Mars – it will not have travelled as far as the Earth around the Sun. The letter M must be on the orbit of Mars.
b(ii)	Any **one** from • outer planets move more slowly • it moves more slowly • outer planets take longer to orbit • Mars has a longer year	1	You will also get the mark if you state that the orbit of Mars is longer or that the outer planets have further to go around their orbit. Mars has a larger orbital path than the Earth and takes 1.9 Earth years to orbit the Sun.
c(i)	A letter V to show that Venus has travelled through more than 90° of its orbit and less than 180°	1	Venus will have travelled further around its orbital path than the Earth in three months. The letter V must be on the orbit of Venus.
c(ii)	Any **one** from • inner planets move more quickly • it moves more quickly • inner planets take less time to orbit • Venus has a shorter year	1	You will also get the mark if you state that the orbit of Venus is shorter or that the inner planets have less far to go around their orbit. Venus has a smaller orbital path than the Earth and takes 0.6 Earth years to orbit the Sun.

LEVEL 7

Question	Answer	Mark	Examiner's comments
1a		2	A pyramid of numbers represents the numbers of each organism at each part of a food chain. The bigger the horizontal bar the larger the numbers of that organism. There are more winter moth caterpillars than oak trees so the first mark is awarded if the second layer is wider than the first. Because the numbers of sparrowhawks is smaller than the number of great tits which is smaller than the number of winter moth caterpillars, the second mark is awarded if the top three layers gradually reduce in size.
b(i)	Any **two** from • sparrowhawks eat great tits which contain insecticide • great tits eat insects which contain insecticide • a sparrowhawk eats lots of great tits **or** each great tit eats lots of caterpillars	2	To get both marks you must explain that animals further down the food chain take in the insecticide and that the quantities of it in animals higher up the food chain increase. When there are two marks for an explanation try to ensure that you make at least two clearly different statements.

	• the insecticide is concentrated at each level in the food chain • insecticide is not easily eliminated • the insecticide is persistent		
b(ii)	Any **one** from • disease • climate change • lack of food **or** water • reduced habitat • fewer great tits	1	You have to give <u>another</u> reason so you will not get the mark if you refer to insecticides. As well as changes to factors that maintain the number of sparrowhawks, you would also get the mark if you suggested the arrival of a new predator or an increase in existing predators.
c(i)	1961 because the number of great tits was highest **or** 1976 because the number of great tits was lowest.	1	Both date and the evidence required for the mark. Both date and the evidence required for the mark.
c(ii)	fewest great tits were eaten **or** less food available for the sparrowhawks	1	The reason given must be linked to the answer given in part c(i).
2a	The factor you would change would be: the metal	1	You may have done an experiment a bit like this or you may not. Remember that doesn't stop you answering the question. You are told Lavoisier's prediction and you know enough about doing experiments to test predictions to work out the answer.
	The factor you would measure to collect results would be: The change in mass of the contents of the crucible after burning.	1	
	The factor you would control could be: To make sure that everything inside the crucible was weighed. To keep a lid on the crucible. To have the same starting mass of metal. To allow enough time for the reaction to occur.	1	Any of these control variables or another sensible suggestion would get the mark.
	The evidence that would support Lavoisier's idea would be: An increase in the mass following burning for all three metals.	1	
b	Your table should have columns for the metal, the mass at the start of burning and the mass at the end of burning and maybe a space for you to work out the change in mass	1	Again you know enough about doing experiments to work this one out even though you might not have done exactly this investigation.
3a(i)	Any **two** from • CO_2 • H_2O • CO • C	2	You are specifically asked for the chemical formulae of the two products. You must use them to get the two marks for this question.
a(ii)	Any **two** from • water droplets form on the inside of the bell-jar • thermal energy is released • light is released • soot is produced • smoke is produced	2	Observations are anything that you can see happening in the bell-jar, which are evidence that a chemical reaction is taking place. You will also get the marks if you refer to condensation on the inside of the jar and that a flame is visible.

b(i)	oxygen increases carbon dioxide decreases	I I	Photosynthesis uses carbon dioxide and produces oxygen. Your answers may be in any order.
b(ii)	photosynthesis stops respiration continues to take place	I I	Photosynthesis requires energy from sunlight to take place. Without this source of energy the process stops.
c(i)	chloroplasts	I	You are expected to know that the green pigment chlorophyll is only found in the chloroplasts of plant cells.
c(ii)	nucleus	I	The nucleus controls all of the functions of the cell.
4a	aluminium oxide	I	Aluminum is more reactive than iron and therefore it reacts with iron oxide to produce aluminium oxide.
b	aluminium iron copper	I	Iron must be more reactive than copper because there is no reaction between iron oxide and copper. The answers must be in the correct order.
c(i)	no reaction	I	Zinc is lower in the list of reactivity than calcium so it will not displace calcium from calcium oxide. Nothing happens when zinc powder is heated with calcium oxide.
c(ii)	Any **one** from • zinc • silver • magnesium	I	Magnesium does not react with magnesium sulphate and neither do zinc and silver because they are both less reactive than magnesium. You will also get the mark here if you use the correct chemical symbol for any of these metals.
d	zinc + oxygen → zinc oxide	2	The word equation has the two reactants zinc and oxygen on the left with the product, zinc oxide on the right.
5a	Any **one** from; • plants subjected to or not subjected to acid • pH of the acid • strength of solution • volume of acid	I	An independent variable is one which is changed during the experiment. These are the factors which you can vary in your laboratory investigation.
b(i)	Any **one** from: • plants live or die • plants healthy or not healthy • plants or leaves change colour • how many seeds grow	I	A dependent variable is one which changes as a result of the changes made to the independent variable during the experimental procedure. Because you have to describe how you could measure this variable, your answer to part (ii) must relate to the dependent variable which you write in this part.
b(ii)	Any **one** from: • number of plants dying/ailing • number of leaves falling/ailing • mass of plant matter • area of plant leaf growth • height of plant	I	Your answer to parts b(i) and b(ii) must relate to the independent variable mentioned in part a.
c	Any **one** from: • soil nutrients • temperature • humidity • light • acidity of soil at the beginning	I	To make sure that what occurs is a direct result of changing the independent variables there are a range of factors which have to be controlled. By doing this you can be sure that they are not causing the changes in the factors (dependent variables) which you are observing or measuring.

6a(i)	magnesium zinc iron copper	1	You must use the pattern of ticks and crosses in the table of results. Copper must be the least reactive because there were no reactions between that metal and the salt solutions of the three other metals. Magnesium must be the most reactive because it displaced the three other metals from the salt solutions. A tick indicates that zinc reacted with iron sulphate. Zinc must, therefore, be more reactive than iron – so zinc is second in the list and iron is third. All four metals must be in the correct order for the mark
a(ii)	<table><tr><td></td><td>Copper</td><td>Iron</td><td>Magnesium</td><td>Zinc</td></tr><tr><td>Copper sulphate</td><td></td><td></td><td></td><td>✓</td></tr><tr><td>Iron sulphate</td><td></td><td></td><td></td><td></td></tr><tr><td>Magnesium sulphate</td><td></td><td>✗</td><td></td><td>✗</td></tr><tr><td>Zinc sulphate</td><td></td><td></td><td></td><td></td></tr></table>	2	Based on the answers to part a(i) – zinc will react with copper sulphate (tick), but neither iron nor zinc will react with magnesium sulphate (crosses). One mark for each correct column.
b(i)	copper nitrate + silver	2	As copper is more reactive it displaces silver from the compound to form copper nitrate and silver. Products may be in any order.
b(ii)	copper silver platinum	1	As platinum does not react with silver nitrate it is less reactive than silver. From part b(i) you know that copper is more reactive than silver.
c	iron because it is more reactive	1	Both the correct name of the metal and reason are required for the mark.
7a(i)	2 N cm	1 1	There is one mark for getting the calculation right and another mark for getting the correct units. It is always important to show units in calculation questions. In this question if you made a mistake with the numbers, showing the correct unit would mean you got half the marks – just the same as the right number without the unit!
(ii)	2 N cm or 'the same'	1	The mobile is balanced so the turning moment from each of the two plastic toys must be equal.
(iii)	0.1	1	Here you can just write the number as the unit is given for you.
b	0.3	1	Here you can just write the number as the unit is given for you.
8a	25	1	Pressure = force/area 175/7 = 25 The unit is not required for the mark as it is given in the question.
b	Any one from • greater than 27 N/cm^2 • greater than the pressure in the tyre	1	The answer must be greater than 27 N/cm^2 as the pressure in the pump must be greater than the pressure in the tyre if air is to be pumped into it.
c	2850	1	Force = pressure x area 30 x 95 = 2850

9a	they will repel/it will push the magnet away/it will push the coil away	I	A magnetic field is produced in the coil when the current flows through it. The end of the coil nearest the North pole of the magnet must be a South pole if they attract each other. When the magnet is turned around, the South pole of the coil will repel the South pole of the magnet.
b(i)	Any **one** from • because the magnet is heavier or the paper clip is lighter • so the moments are equal	I	The magnet is heavy and a short distance from the pivot. To balance it the paper clip, which is lighter than the magnet, must be placed further from the pivot.
b(ii)	current in the coil produces a magnetic field the magnet is attracted/repelled	I I	The magnetic field produced around the coil when the current flows interacts with the magnetic field of the magnet. The resulting force causes the magnet to move.
b(iii)	Any **one** from • the straw is deflected more or moves more • the reading is higher or goes up Any **one** from • it increases the magnetic field • it makes the electromagnet stronger • it attracts or repels the magnet more strongly	I I	The soft iron in the middle of the coil concentrates the magnetic field increasing the force being applied to the magnet. The force between the coil and the magnet is greater and the reading on the scale is higher.

Glossary

absorb To take in, e.g. some materials absorb water.

accuracy A measure of the quality of the measurements taken in an experiment.

acid A solution with a pH value less than 7.

acid rain Rain which has a pH value less than 7 because it has dissolved pollutants from the air.

adaptation Any characteristic that enables the survival of an organism in its environment.

aerobic respiration A series of chemical reactions that use oxygen to produce energy from glucose in living cells.

alkali A solution with a pH value greater than 7.

alloy A solid mixture of two or more metals.

amplitude The maximum deflection of a wave from its centre line.

angle of incidence The angle that a ray of light makes with the normal to a surface.

angle of reflection The angle from the normal at which a ray of light is reflected from a surface.

anther The part of the stamen which produces pollen.

antibodies Produced by the immune system to attack bacteria and viruses.

atom The smallest part of an element that can take part in a chemical reaction.

bacteria Single-celled organisms that cause illnesses like pneumonia and cholera.

balanced diet The range of foods that provides the proteins, carbohydrates, fat, vitamins and minerals that the body needs to stay healthy.

battery An energy source for electrical circuits.

biomass The body tissues of an organism.

boiling The rapid change of state from a liquid to a gas.

boiling point The temperature at which a liquid boils.

burning A vigorous reaction between a fuel and oxygen, producing heat and light.

carbohydrates A food group that includes starch and sugars.

carbon dioxide Produced by burning fossil fuels. It forms an insulating layer in the atmosphere leading to the greenhouse effect.

carnivore An animal that eats other animals.

carpel The female part of a flower consisting of the stigma, style and ovary.

cell The building block of all life. An energy store; can be joined to make batteries.

cell membrane The surface that surrounds a cell and holds everything inside. It also determines which materials can and cannot enter the cell.

cell sap The watery solution contained within cells.

cell wall A tough, protective outer layer of a plant cell.

chemical change A change which is difficult to reverse and where the products are different to the reactants.

chemical formula Symbols used to show which and how many atoms of chemical elements make up a chemical compound.

chemical reaction A change where the products are different from the starting chemicals.

chemical symbol The letters used to represent chemical elements.

chemical weathering The breakdown of rocks caused by a chemical reaction.

chlorophyll The green pigment in plants which traps light energy for use in photosynthesis.

chloroplast Structures found only in plant cells which contain chlorophyll.

chromatography A separation method that relies on the different solubilities of substances in a solvent.

chromosome Coils of DNA found in all cell nuclei that carry the information needed to make an organism.

circuit A complete loop of electrical components and connecting wires around which electrical charge can flow.

classification Sorting organisms into related groups.

combustion The reaction that happens when any substance burns in oxygen.

compound A substance containing more than one type of atom chemically combined.

compress To squeeze something.

conclusion The decision reached after examining the data from an experiment.

condensation A change of state from a gas to a liquid.

consumer An organism that eats a producer or another consumer. All animals are consumers.

contract Get smaller.

current A flow of electrical charge around a circuit.

cytoplasm The jelly-like part of a cell where many chemical reactions take place.

digestion Breaking down large, complex substances in your food, into smaller, simpler substances that can be absorbed into your blood.

dissolving When a substance forms a solution in a solvent. Dissolving is reversible.

distillation Separating a mixture of liquids by boiling one of them and then condensing it elsewhere.

DNA The substance responsible for transmitting genetic information.

electrical conductivity The extent to which a material will allow electrical charge to flow through it.

element A substance made from only one type of atom.

energy The ability to do work.

environment The area in which an organism lives or the surrounding conditions.

evaporation Changing state from liquid to gas at a temperature lower than the liquid's boiling point.

expand Get bigger.

fats The energy-rich food group contained within vegetable oils and dairy products.

fertilisation When male and female nuclei fuse to create a complete set of instructions for a new organism.

fetus A baby forming in its mother's uterus when cells start to become specialised.

fibre Mostly undigested plant material which helps food to move through your digestive system.

filament The stalk of a stamen.

filtration Separating an insoluble solid from a liquid by pouring the mixture through a filter paper. The filtrate passes through the paper but the solid residue is left behind.

filtrate The liquid that passes through a filter.

flower The reproductive part of a flowering plant.

food chain A series of feeding relationships.

food web A series of related food chains.

force A force pushes objects together or pulls them apart.

fossil fuels Fuels made from the fossilised remains of living things.

fractional distillation Separating a mixture of liquids using their different boiling points to boil one liquid off at a time.

freezing Changing state from a liquid into a solid.

frequency The number of waves that pass a point in a second. Frequency is measured in hertz (Hz).

fuel A material that burns to release energy.

fungi The largest micro-organism. The mould on rotting food is an example.

gametes Reproductive cells with a single set of chromosomes capable of joining with another gamete of the other sex from which a new organism develops.

gas A state of matter. Particles in a gas move freely and are far apart from each other. A gas will fill its container and can be compressed easily.

geothermal energy Energy produced using the heat of the Earth's rocks.

global warming This is caused by the increase in the greenhouse effect due to increased levels of carbon dioxide in the atmosphere.

glucose The sugar made during photosynthesis.

gravity The force of attraction between two objects.

greenhouse effect The trapping of light energy within the Earth's atmosphere by gases. This warms the Earth's atmosphere.

groups Collections of materials or living things which have similar properties.

guard cells Cells that open and close stomata.

habitat The area where an organism lives.

herbivore An animal that only eats plants.

hydroelectric power Electricity that is generated by moving water.

igneous rock Rock made from cooling molten rock (magma).

immune system The system in the body that produces antibodies.

immunisation A method of making the body produce antibodies to fight diseases.

incident ray Ray of light moving towards an object.

indicator A substance that shows whether a solution is an acid or alkali by a colour change.

inheritance Passing on genetic information from adult to offspring.

insoluble Does not dissolve in a particular solvent.

insulator Any material that does not easily let heat or electrical charge flow through it.

invertebrates Animals that do not have a backbone.

key A set of questions or statements used to identify living things.

large intestine Part of your gut where water from food is absorbed into your blood.

laterally inverted An image with sides apparently the opposite way round to the sides of the object.

liquid A state of matter. A liquid's particles are free to move and close together. Liquids are difficult to compress and take the shape of their container.

luminous Something that gives out light.

machine A device used to do work.

magma Molten rock, from inside the Earth.

magnet An object that can attract a piece of iron. Magnets can attract or repel other magnets.

magnetic field The area around a magnet where the force of the magnet can be detected.

magnetic field lines Lines drawn around a magnet to show where the magnetic field is.

mammals The class of vertebrate animals which incudes humans.

mass The amount of matter that an object is made of. Mass is measured in kilograms or grams.

melting Changing state from a solid to a liquid.

melting point Temperature at which a solid melts.

metamorphic rock Rock formed when other rocks are heated and squashed in the Earth's crust.

micro–organism An organism only visible using a microscope.

mitochondria The tiny mobile structures within cells where aerobic respiration takes place.

mixture Two or more elements or compounds that are not chemically joined together.

molecule Two or more atoms chemically joined together, the atoms could be the same or different.

Moon The only natural satellite orbiting the Earth.

neutral solutions Solutions with a pH of 7.

newton The S.I. unit of force.

non-renewable energy source An energy source that cannot be replaced once it has been used.

normal A line at 90° to the surface of an object.

north seeking pole The pole of a bar magnet that points towards the Earth's magnetic north pole.

nuclear energy Energy produced when particles of uranium split.

nucleus The control centre of a cell.

offspring New animals or plants resulting from reproduction.

omnivore An animal that eats plants and animals.

opaque A description of materials which do not allow light to pass through them.

orbit The path an object follows as it moves around another object.

ore A rock that contains a useful mineral.

organ Part of an organism which is specialised for a particular function.

organ system A collection of organs which all have a role in one particular biological process.

oscilloscope A piece of equipment used to display a range of waveforms.

ovary Part of the female reproductive system where female sex cells (ova in animals and ovules in plants) develop.

ovule The female sex cell of a plant.

ovum The female sex cell of an animal.

oxidation A reaction where a substance combines with oxygen.

oxide A compound of oxygen with another element.

parallel Two things extending in the same direction as each other and remaining the same distance apart.

parallel circuit An electrical circuit in which there are two or more possible routes for the current to flow along.

particle model A useful set of ideas concerning a small body that helps us to understand some of the things that happen to substances.

petals Brightly coloured leaves of a flower.

pH A measure of the acidity or alkalinity of a liquid or solution of a solid.

photosynthesis The process by which plants make glucose from water and carbon dioxide using sunlight.

physical change The reversible change of a substance from one state to another.

physical weathering The breakdown of rocks caused by a physical process.

pitch How high or low a note is.

pivot The point on which something is able to turn.

pollen Grains that hold the male sex cells of plants.

pollination Transfer of pollen from the anther of one flower to the stigma of another.

primary consumers Animals which eat plants.

producer An organism that traps energy to make glucose. Plants are the producers for most of the Earth's food chains.

products Substances made as a result of chemical reactions.

protein The food group that gives us the chemicals we need to grow and repair our bodies.

protozoa Micro-organisms that cause diseases such as malaria and amoebic dysentery.

pure Containing only one type of particle.

pyramid of numbers A diagram showing the number of organisms at each level of a food chain.

radiation Any of the different types of electromagnetic wave.

random Without any pattern or organisation.

reactants Substances which react with each other.

reduction The loss of oxygen during a chemical reaction.

reflect To bounce back from a surface.

reflected ray A ray of light reflected from a surface.

refraction When light changes direction as it passes into and out of a transparent object.

relay switch A switch in a circuit that, when it is closed, acts as the switch for another circuit.

reliability The measure of how repeatable the results from an experiment are.

renewable energy source An energy source that does not run out, such as wind, water or Sun.

reproduction Making offspring. Humans reproduce when they have babies.

respiration Releasing energy in cells through a chemical reaction.

reversible Can be changed back.

root hair cells Cells near the tip of a root that have hair-like extensions to absorb water.

saliva Produced by glands in the mouth, it wets food and contains amylase to start to digest starch.

secondary colour A colour made by combining two or more primary colours.

secondary consumers Animals that eat primary consumers.

sedimentary rock Rocks made when a sediment is squashed and becomes cemented together.

series circuit An electrical circuit in which all the components are lined up one after the other for the current to pass through.

sex chromosomes The chromosomes that make you male or female.

sexual reproduction The process of producing new individuals as the result of the combination of both male and female genetic information.

shadows Dark patches made on a surface when an object stops light getting to the surface.

small intestine Part of the gut where digestion is finished and food particles are absorbed into your blood.

Solar System The complete collection of asteroids, planets and comets moving around the Sun.

solid A state of matter. In a solid, particles are in fixed positions. The particles cannot move around freely but they can vibrate. The particles are close together so solids cannot be easily compressed.

solution A mixture of a solute and a solvent in which the substances are not chemically combined.

solvent A liquid that dissolves a solute.

specialised Adapted for a particular function.

species A grouping of organisms which can breed successfully.

sperm A male sex cell of an animal.

stamen The male parts of a flower (the anther and filament).

starch A carbohydrate made up of sugar molecules chemically joined **together.**

states of matter Solid, liquid and gas are the three states of matter. The state that a substance is in depends mainly upon its temperature.

stigma The sticky female part of a flower where pollen gets caught.

stomach The part of your gut where digestion of protein happens.

stomata Holes in the surfaces of leaves, mostly on the underside, used for the exchange of gases.

style The part of the carpel between the ovary and the stigma.

substance A material that only contains one type of particle. A substance is always pure because a pure material only has one type of particle.

sulphur dioxide Produced by burning fossil fuels. It can cause acid rain.

Sun Our nearest star; the centre of the Solar System.

switch A component which is used to make and break an electrical circuit easily.

symbol (electrical) Used to represent components in an electrical circuit diagram.

symbol equation A summary of a chemical reaction using symbols only.

thermal conductivity The measure of how easily thermal energy passes through a material.

translucent Allowing some light to pass through.

transparent A material that lets most light falling on to it to pass through.

trend A general pattern in data or behaviour.

Universal Indicator A mixture of indicators which gives a definite colour change for each whole change of pH value from 1 to 14.

uterus The part of the female reproductive system where a baby develops.

vacuole Structures containing cell sap found in plant cells. Vacuoles help plant cells to stay rigid and the plant to stay upright.

variation The difference between individuals within a species.

vertebrate An animal that has a backbone.

villi Finger-like projections on the small intestine wall. Villi make the surface area much bigger so that more food substances can be absorbed into the blood.

virtual image An image that appears to exist but cannot be caught on a screen.

virus The smallest micro-organism responsible for diseases such as 'flu, measles and chicken pox.

wavefronts Imaginary lines joining points at the same position on a series of waves.

wavelength The distance between the same point on two successive waves.

waves The movement of energy from one place to another without the particles of the medium being permanently displaced.

weight The pulling force of the Earth's gravity on an object. Weight tells you how heavy something is. Weight is measured in newtons (N).

white blood cells Cells in your blood that fight off invading micro-organisms by engulfing them or making antibodies to kill them.

wind The horizontal movement of air over the Earth's surface.

wind energy Energy produced from the wind moving the blades attached to an aerogenerator.

word equation A summary of a chemical reaction using only words.

xylem Cells that are adapted for the transportation of water through a plant.

Index